Positively Canadian

A FUN GUIDE TO
CANADIAN LANGUAGE, CULTURE AND HISTORY

D1413962

Heather Ann
Pattullo

Tellwell Talent
www.tellwell.ca

ISBN
978-0-9952663-0-8 (Paperback)
978-0-9952663-2-2 (eBook)

Contents

Dedication

This book is written in memory of my mother, Edythe ("Anne") Dean McCallum, for whose insistence on my using proper English I have always been grateful.

I happily dedicate this book to my six "Grands:" 3 Canadians – Hannah, Benjamin and Noah, and 3 Texans – Kirsten, Josiah, and Jacob – for having 'tolerated' my correcting their English from their early years.

As "Positively Canadian" goes to print, I am reminded how each chapter is a reflection of my love for this treasured homeland. If each reader—whether new to Canada or a long-time resident—will come to know and love this great nation just a little more, the book will have fulfilled its purpose.

With great anticipation, I dedicate "Positively Canadian" to Canada on its 150th birthday.

Happy Birthday Canada!
Bonne Fête Canada!

Acknowledgements

I have enjoyed writing this book but I could not have withstood all the "blank walls" and "rabbit holes of research" without the solid friendship of the unique "AAA" (Aspiring Artists and Authors) mentorship group. Connie, Jane and Elin; our encouraging luncheon discussions and your unfailing belief in my actually completing "the book" are immeasurable. To have your beautiful flowers in the book is such a 'bonus,' Jane!

Another "bonus" was finding the great detailed maps here:

   bruce@bjdesign.com

From the first online connection, to phone calls and Skype time, Bruce Jones has given me service beyond measure. He made sure the maps not only reflect what I wanted but also that they were in the form that was needed for publication.

I owe heart-felt thanks to Charmaine Chiu, my charming high school student, who worked over the summer to do all sorts of "computer magic" and add specific place names to the maps. It was clear that this was not my area of expertise!

To my friend and author, Cynthia Elizabeth ("Cynny") Sully, I give huge thanks for sharing her experiences and helping me dip my toes into the unknown world of publishing.

Special thanks also to all my friends across the country who took time to comment on chapter drafts and add interesting bits from their experiences (and who corrected me when I had the St. Lawrence River flowing the wrong way!)

For my dear friend, life coach, and incomparable woman of wisdom, Nancy Carlstrom, the word 'thanks' cannot encompass my gratitude. I deeply appreciate all the hours of "tweaking suggestions," direction and encouragement you have given me from the time this 'book' was just a wisp of a dream. Your patience has no end and you are indeed a special "gem."

Extra special thanks to my family who have allowed me the space to pursue this dream – to step away from our family USANA Health Sciences business this past year – and to miss special family times and grandsons' hockey games to attend book-writing seminars and workshops.

Last but absolutely not least, my love and thanks to Gary, my loyal supporter over 50 years of marriage. Your mother would be so proud of the "cook" you have become as you slipped into that unaccustomed role so we wouldn't starve while I wrote, and wrote. When you have this book in your hands, Gary Bear, I promise to make a scrumptious meal to go with it!

Introduction

I have always wanted to write a book. Yes, always! I made several unsuccessful writing attempts in my teens and finally just became a voracious reader instead. The dream dimmed, but never died.

During my years as a nursing professor, I became aware of the difficulty that 3rd year university students with English as a second language were having with written work. I remember learning that students who had not been born in Canada – and even some who had – knew very little about this fascinating country. Little did I know the idea for this very book was being formed!

After I retired from teaching, I attended a "how-to-write-a-book" seminar. That quickly fanned my book-writing flame and my dream was re-ignited! The gem I took away from that day was "If you want to write a book, you have to write something about which you are passionate!"

I realized I had two passions and suddenly, they blended together and became a theme. I love Canada and I am passionate about using good English. I could write a small book that would help not only ESL students but also new Canadians improve their English and learn about Canada in the process.

I met with wonderful groups of students studying in Vancouver who shared with me some of the joys and frustrations of coming to a foreign country to study English. They definitely assisted me to make the content of this book much more relevant and, I trust, also more interesting to you, my readers.

As you begin to read, imagine we are having an interesting conversation – you and I. I have included some of my own comments and some 'zany' facts about this wonderful country to make the "exercises" interesting. The truth is, it's impossible to include every interesting place in each province/territory and I am just hoping to spark your curiosity. I'm trusting you will do your own research for the unique things you find in this book that you want to explore further. Canada is a young nation but it has such compelling history!

I enjoyed my years of teaching, interacting with students, and the fun we had discovering facts and sharing interesting experiences. We definitely shared a love of learning.

Now I'm sharing this love of learning with you. It's the enjoyment of discovering new facts and sharing my experiences, as well as new learning from the grammar exercises, that is waiting for you in this book. It has been written with enthusiasm and passion from my heart to yours.

Why "Canada"? A Bit of History

How did Canada get its name?

I love Canada! I love its history, the splendor of its scenery and the cultural mosaic of its people. I just love being a Canadian!

I can't imagine saying "I love being a Tuponian" or a "Hochelagender" – can you?

Tuponia and Hochelaga were some names suggested back in the 1800s to call this magnificent land. The name *Canada* probably came from the Aboriginal word *kanata* meaning "village," "settlement" or "land." After

1

the French explorer Jacques Cartier's visits in the 1530s, European books and maps began referring to this region as Canada. The name stuck and was formally adopted at the Confederation meeting in Charlottetown, Prince Edward Island, in 1867 – the meeting that officially created the country, Canada.

It's easy to think that Jacques Cartier and Samuel de Champlain in the 1500s were the first European explorers of Canada but they were not! The Vikings explored here first! Consider the 1000 year-old site of L'Anse aux Meadows in Newfoundland. In the 1960s, evidence of a Viking village was discovered, making it the oldest historical site in Canada.

What's great about that site is that we can view a few of the *original* foundation walls. However, all the rest has been left buried. We can stand in *replicas* of the sod buildings that the Vikings built. *(I love feeling like we can slip back in time to over 1000 years ago.)*

Replicas of the Viking sod homes excavated in the 1960's *(Photo courtesy of Paul Illsley)*

Aboriginal Groups and Explorers

Early explorers, such as Cartier and Champlain, met only a few different Aboriginal groups in their travels. Actually, there were many well-established Aboriginal nations in this vast land between the Atlantic and Pacific Oceans. At first, the Europeans lumped them all together as "savages" but other explorers quickly discovered there were, in fact, *many nations* of Aboriginal groups. They had adapted to this land over tens of thousands of years.

These native nations spoke different languages and dialects. They organized their societies and governments differently, developed distinctive cultures and economies, and made their own specific adaptations to climate and landscape. Many of the explorers, and later the settlers, owed their lives to Aboriginal knowledge of how to heal sicknesses and how to adapt to Canada's hostile weather. *(For an explorer to survive a Canadian winter without freezing to death was a major success!)*

Europeans were certainly not all similar either. There were fishermen who sailed to Newfoundland to cure cod, whalers who sailed into the Arctic, and explorers who charted the waterways of the continent. Many came looking for a "shortcut" to China (Cathay) they called a "northwest passage." They all came from different lands, such as Portugal, Spain France and Britain.

France and Britain Claimed Canada

Cartier claimed the new land he had 'discovered' for France, but the British had also landed, and had begun to claim land for the King of England! Back in their homelands, France and Britain were engaged in a Seven Years War (1756-1763) and this war was also being played out in Canada.

In 1759, there was a big battle on the Plains of Abraham overlooking what is now Québec City. The British, under General James Wolfe, conquered the French under General Louis-Joseph de Montcalm. Both generals were killed finally ending the Seven Years War. It is the result of this battle to which French Canadians refer with the words on their Québec license plates "Je me souviens" – I remember. You will read a bit more about this in the Québec Chapter.

There are many more interesting facts about how Canada "survived" the Seven Years War. It is interesting to discover why the removal of France as a North American power led indirectly to the American Revolution. You may read more here:

thecanadianencyclopedia.ca/en/article/seven-years-war/

After the American Revolution (1775-1783), the American colonies were no longer governed by Britain. Many settlers in these colonies, who were loyal to Britain, moved into the Québec and Ontario area. This area was split in 1791 into Lower and Upper Canada, but in 1841, they merged to become the Province of Canada. Then, New Brunswick and Nova Scotia joined it in 1867 at Confederation to form the country of Canada. A capital city for the new country – chosen by Queen Victoria - was built in Ottawa. *(Prince Edward Island hadn't decided if joining Canada had any benefits so they did not join!)*

Explorers moved west to the Rocky Mountains and up to the Arctic Ocean in 1870. Finally, with the addition of British Columbia in 1871, Canada extended "from sea to sea." This became Canada's motto: *A mari usque ad mare.* But wait a minute – what about Newfoundland, Canada's most easterly province? It took until **1949** to convince Newfoundland that they just *might* benefit from joining confederation! *(Newfoundlanders have always been seriously independent, eh?)* For Canada's provinces to be *really* joined from the Atlantic to the Pacific, it took the building of a railway. If British Columbia would join Confederation, the Prime Minister, Sir John A. Macdonald, promised to build a railway to the Pacific coast. *(When you get to the British Columbia Chapter you'll find out how long it took to finish the promised railway!)*

Immigration

Canada's original inhabitants were the Aboriginals whose ancestors migrated across the Bering Strait from Asia over 10,000 years ago. From the 1500s on, immigrants came from around the world to settle in this "new world." Canada has opened its doors to people from Ireland to escape the potato famine (1845-1852) and from Ukraine to escape blights and famine (1890s). In the late 1800s and early 1900's, thousands of Chinese workers came to build the railway across this vast country.

People from the British Isles have been coming since the 1600s to settle on Canadian farmland and to help build cities. The United States describes its people groups as a "melting pot;" Canada refers to the different cultures as forming a "mosaic" of different languages and traditions. Although English and French are the two "official" languages of Canada, you will hear the "Scottish burr" in Nova Scotia or an "Irish lilt" in Ontario. You would definitely hear Ukrainian spoken in Manitoba and Alberta and many British accents as well as Mandarin, Punjabi and Hindi spoken in British Columbia.

A very interesting story about post-war immigration in the 1940s is about the 45,000 "War Brides" who came to Canada. They had married Canadian soldiers and had said good-bye to their homes in England, France, or Italy to come and live in Canada. You may read about them here: canadianwarbrides.com/intro.asp

I am pleased that Canada has been one of the world's first countries to welcome 25,000 refugees fleeing persecution in Syria and other war-ravaged countries. I hope they will come to love Canada as I do. No matter where they have come from, it doesn't take long for immigrants to call Canada home. They are the reason Canada has emerged as a thriving country and one of the best places in the world to live. *(Have you ever had an experience as a refugee? I haven't. However, I remember feeling very uncomfortable as an English person to live and work in northern Québec when I was not yet fluent in French.)*

Canada Today

In the 2011 Census, Aboriginal peoples in Canada totaled 1,400,685 or 4.3% of the national population. They include over 600 recognized First Nations governments or Bands with distinctive cultures, languages, art, and music.

Canada, today, is a land rich in natural resources and rich in the diverse cultures of its over 35,000,000 people. We have industrialists, farmers, artists, factory workers, health care providers, scientists, miners, educational institutions and an infrastructure that is the envy of many other nations.

Oh yes, I must not forget we also have some of the world's greatest hockey players of the last 50 years – Maurice "Rocket" Richard, Bobby Orr, Clarke, Henderson, "the Great Gretzky," Trottier, Fuhr, Murphy, Messier, Robitaille, Gallagher, Yzerman, Price, Howe, McDonald, LaFleur and Crosby – just to name a few. I hope you are getting a sense of our multicultural heritage as you read the names of those born-in-Canada hockey players? ☺ Canadians *really* love hockey, possibly because we say the game was invented in Canada. ALSO, although the USA has over 314 million people to choose from, and Canada has only 35 million, we can still produce some of the best hockey players in the world! *N'est ce pas?*

We also have world-renown authors, musicians and artists. To learn more of the history of Canada, check out Pierre Berton's books. To read novels with a Québec perspective, find Gabrielle Roy's books. To read about the Prairies, try books by Sharon Butala and Margaret Laurence. Find the hilarious books by Farley Mowat from Newfoundland. The paintings of the Group of Seven can be seen in the art galleries of the world. If you listen to opera you would enjoy the well-loved British Columbia tenor, Ben Hepner. If you prefer popular music, how about Céline Dion, or the group with the original name "Bare Naked Ladies"? Then there's good ol' Hank Snow for country and western songs; Gordon Lightfoot and Anne Murray for some folksongs, and Michael Bublé and Shania Twain for a range of well-loved tunes.

The paintings of the Group of Seven (formed in 1920) can be seen in the art galleries of the world. The work of Tom Thomson influenced these artists but he died tragically in 1917. You can read more here:

thecanadianencyclopedia.ca/en/article/tom-thomson/
(I really wanted you to see the blue in this painting. Isn't it awesome!)

In the Northland (1915) by Tom Thomson

Friends Across the Border

The border between Canada and the United States is referred to as the "longest undefended border in the world." The War of 1812 (1812-14) was the last time we were at war with each other. Of course, at that time, we were really "the British" fighting against anti-British "revolutionaries" to the south. From then on, we have fought side by side in two world wars. We now generally rely on mutual defense in the western hemisphere. A plaque on a monument on Belle Isle, an island in the Detroit River between Michigan, USA and Canada, notes our close ties with these words:

Dedicated to the Glory of God and in the hope of everlasting peace between the peoples of the Dominion of Canada and of the United States of America. AD 1941

Did you know ...

* It was during the war of 1812, that the poem "The Star Spangled Banner" was written by Francis Scott Key. It became the USA National Anthem – but not until 1931.

* The distinctive red and white Canadian maple leaf flag was raised for the first time on February 15, 1965, at hundreds of ceremonies across the country and around the world. It replaced the British flag – but only with great debate! *(I remember the excitement! We finally had a flag of our own!...Perhaps you have had a similar experience?)*

* The **C**anadian **N**ational **R**ailway was extended from "sea to sea" by absorbing several small railways across Canada. By the early 1920's, there were 2 railways taking people and goods across Canada.

* Canada and USA were the first countries to sign The **North Atlantic Treaty Organization (NATO)** created in 1949. This group will help defend each member country if attacked by any external party. NATO's headquarters are in Brussels, Belgium, one of the 28 member states across North America and Europe.

* In May 1958, Canada and USA created the **North American Aerospace Defense Command (NORAD]**. This provides aerospace warning, air sovereignty, and defense for North America. The NORAD command center is located at Peterson Air Force Base in Colorado, USA. *(This was the era of the "Cold War." You can find lots online to learn about these years.)*

* If you are in Vancouver and want to see the spectacular Rocky Mountains, you would travel on the Rocky Mountaineer Railway or on VIA Rail. From these trains, you would see some of the most breathtaking scenery in British Columbia and Alberta.

* Building a railway helped settle and develop Western Canada. Canada's first Prime Minister, Sir John A. Macdonald, promised British Columbia

when it entered Confederation in 1871 that a railway would extend from Montréal, Québec to New Westminster, BC. In 1885, the last spike was driven and that **C**anadian **P**acific **R**ailway remains a symbol of national unity in Canada. You can read more about it in two of Pierre Berton's exciting books about Canada – *The National Dream* and *The Last Spike*.

**The first Transcontinental Train to go from
the Atlantic to the Pacific - 1886**

* Adelaide Hoodless was a feisty woman concerned about the poor health of women and children in Ontario. She told the Farmers' Institute in 1897 that the men took more interest in the health of their animals than the health of their families! She insisted women should have an Institute of their own. One week later, in Stoney Creek, Ontario, over 100 women attended the founding meeting of the first **W**omen's **I**nstitute. Now there are 8.5 million members worldwide! *(My aunt, a WI member, told me women isolated in rural Canada loved the WI where they could socialize while learning how to improve their family's health. Way to go, Adelaide!)*

* *Cirque du Soleil* is a dramatic mix of circus arts and high quality, artistic entertainment. It was first presented in 1984 during Québec's 450th anniversary celebration of Jacques Cartier's discovery of Canada. The troop constantly seeks to "evoke the imagination, invoke the senses and provoke the emotions of people around the world." *(I knew my 9 year-old grand-son, Noah, would enjoy this phenomenal show, but I wasn't so sure about his 15 year-old brother. When I peeked over at Ben, I saw he was completely mesmerized! What a special, magical night! Be sure to see this group!)*

Newfoundland and Labrador
Provincial Flower

Pitcher Plant

Jane Crosby, 2014, watercolour 24 x 14 cm

2

Newfoundland and Labrador (NL)
– "Canada's Best-kept Secret"

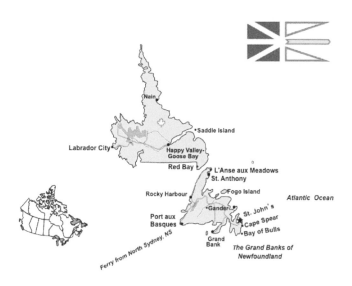

Newfoundland and Labrador has two separate land masses – Newfoundland, which is an island, and Labrador, which is part of the Canadian mainland.

<u>Population</u>: 541,000 (2011)   <u>Joined Confederation</u>: March 31, 1949

<u>Main Cities</u>: St. John's (Capital), Corner Brook, Deer Lake, Labrador City

<u>Places to Visit/Things to See</u>:

Gros Morne National Park   Marble Mountain
L'Anse aux Meadows   Royal St. John's Regatta
Signal Hill   Bay of Bulls

Newfoundland and Labrador is Canada's most easterly province that hugs the Atlantic Ocean. Almost 98% of the people have English as their mother tongue. *(Not a lot of immigrants have settled in Newfoundland!)*

History

When the first Europeans arrived, several Aboriginal groups – the Innu and the Inuit - had been living on the land for thousands of years. The Beothuks were probably the Aboriginals first encountered by the Vikings. Unlike other Aboriginal tribes, they withdrew and did not trade with the European explorers. They did, however, have many unsuccessful skirmishes with the white settlers and also the Mi'kmaq who came from Nova Scotia. They did not survive in isolation and the last known Beothuk died in 1829. You can learn more here:

heritage.nf.ca/aboriginal/beothuk.html

For almost a century after John Cabot explored Newfoundland, fishers and whalers came to the province. Fishing boats from England, France, Spain, and Portugal would haul in enormous catches of cod every summer. In 1583, despite the presence of fishing boats from many European countries, Sir Humphrey Gilbert claimed the Newfoundland territory for England. *(I guess other explorers decided not to claim it first so he did!)*

The first new settlers to Newfoundland were the English, Irish, French and some Scots. The first settlers were isolated a long time from the rest of Canada. Thus, they were outside the mainstream of social, political, and economic development. Having no roads to connect villages, many different spoken dialects developed. Also, they had about 300 years to create their own way of expressing themselves in English! I love their terms of endearment, such as "ducky" (for a female friend or relative) and "b'y" (meaning boy and used for friends), and their use of 'right' and 'some' to mean "very." For example, "She's some pretty!" or "He's a right handy b'y!"

I think this province is Canada's best-kept secret! Growing up in the Maritimes, I often heard the province referred to as "The Rock" by many who live along its rocky shores. Today, many dislike the term so with utmost respect I don't use it now. Also, during my growing up years, Newfoundlanders were often affectionately called "Newfies" – especially when we heard their distinctive lilting accent in other parts of Canada. However, times have changed, and the term is not appreciated by many of today's Newfoundland residents. These days I only use it with my closest NL friends who know I mean it as a term of endearment. When travelling in NL, I suggest we take our cue from the residents whether or not to use these terms.

The home of Wilfred Grenfell has been preserved in St. Anthony on the northern tip of the island. He was the British doctor who came to the island in 1892. When he saw the fishermen living in poverty and poor health, he stayed and served them for over 50 years. He wrote several books about his time in Newfoundland and Labrador. *(His real life scary adventure, "Adrift on an Ice-Pan," reads like a 'reality television' episode!)*

(Do you remember when it cost 5 cents to mail a letter? I certainly don't!)

Newfoundland Today

Newfoundland English can sound very different and it's sometimes difficult to pick up the meaning of a sentence the first time! Some of the expressions are very unique. Here are some examples:

"That rock usually bes underwater." (That rock is usually under water.)

"Where me hat gone to?" (Where is my hat?)

"Drop over me 'ouse we haves a cup of tea." (Come to my house for a cup of tea.)

"Stay where you're to and I'll come where you're at." (Stay there and I'll come to you!) *(I even say that sometimes just to pretend I speak "Newfoundland English"!)*

My own experience was listening to my friend tell me a story about the time he came down the Gander River in his homemade boat. What I heard was:

> "I mind the time I comes down dis river wit a oil eater in my boat. It flopped dis way and dat and I thot she was goin' over"!

I pictured a big fish flopping around in the boat! What he meant was, he had an <u>oil heater</u> in the boat that banged around a lot and nearly went over the side! I quickly learned that residents of Newfoundland and Labrador like to drop the first 'h' in a word and add it onto the next word. *(Keeps us on our toes, eh?)* Search a few YouTube videos to hear some unique Newfoundland phrases.

One of Canada's largest ferries travels between Sydney, Nova Scotia and Port aux Basques, Newfoundland. From this southwest corner of the island it's a 900 km drive to the city of St. John's on the island's southeast corner. Tourists enjoy the many shops and museums in St. John's and the crafts found in little villages sprinkled along the coast.

This province has hundreds of harbours, but perhaps the most well known is in the capital city of St. John's. You can still see the anchor bolts in the huge rocks on each side of the harbour. They secured the nets that were stretched across it to prevent German U-boats from entering during WW II. *(I have a friend whose father used to open the nets to let the Allies' boats into the harbour.)* About 40% of Newfoundlanders live in this area.

Gros Morne National Park is a world heritage site on Newfoundland's west coast. The mountains that line the beautiful Western Brook Pond (a fresh water fjord) are not peaked like the Rockies in British Columbia. That's because their tops have been worn down over the last 1.2 billion years. The Rockies are a mere 800 million years old. *(Just 800 million years? They are just youngsters! Have you travelled to the Rockies? They are spectacular!)*

Colourful houses "stepping down" to St. John's Harbour

At the tip of the northern peninsula is L'Anse aux Meadows with replicas of the Vikings' sod shelters, and the small village of St. Anthony. If it's the right time of year you might see some icebergs! *(I saw two HUGE ones when I was there! Absolutely 'awesome!'! Have you seen icebergs close up?)*

Before leaving there are a few things you *must* do. They include chewing the delicious saltwater taffy; having a jigs dinner (corn beef and cabbage); taking a tour to see the puffins, and becoming an Honorary Newfoundlander by having a "Screech In " ceremony. *(Such fun!)*

For many years, Newfoundland and Labrador experienced a depressed economy. Following the collapse of the cod fishery during the early 1990s, there were very high rates of unemployment and the population decreased drastically. The good news is that in recent years there has been a major energy and resources boom. This has been seen especially in mining and the IT industry. Tourism has increased greatly as tourists find an amazing variety of things to see and do. Many head for Marble Mountain to ski and go zip lining. Others like to watch for whales in the Bay of Bulls. Hopefully, they don't leave "Canada's best kept secret" without trying a jiggs dinner with figgy duff! *(That's a boiled dinner of salt beef and veggies with steamed, spicy bread pudding. Recipe online!)*

The very cute Atlantic Puffins

Labrador

Labrador is the distinct, northerly region of the province of Newfoundland and Labrador. It is actually the mainland portion of the province, separated from the island by the Strait of Belle Isle. It is the largest and northernmost geographical region in Atlantic Canada. It occupies the eastern part of the Labrador Peninsula and is bordered to the west and the south by the Canadian province of Québec. This area has 29,000 km of coastline and 7,000 tiny islands. *(You'll never run out of places to explore!)*

History

The Aboriginal peoples of Labrador have lived there for many thousands of years. From the 1500s, there were many non-Aboriginal settlers and fishermen along the coast. In the mid-16th century, whalers from the Basque region of France and Spain braved the month-long journey across the Atlantic to hunt whales. They established a "rendering plant" on Saddle Island at Red Bay. Situated on this southern tip of Labrador for over 70 years, it produced the whale oil that lit the lamps of Europe. *(I never knew that! Did you?)*

A Spanish galleon, possibly the *San Juan* that had sunk in 1565, was found submerged in Red Bay Harbour in 1978. Archeologists have found the remains of buildings and a Basque whalers' cemetery. In 2013, the Red Bay Basque Whaling Station in Labrador was named Canada's 17th UNESCO World Heritage site.

A Basque whalers' chalupa recovered from the waters of Red Bay

Fishermen from Poole, England settled Battle Harbour in the 1790s, and Dr. Grenfell established a hospital and settled there in 1892. For two centuries it was the economic and social centre of the southeastern Labrador coast. Now it is a wonderful tourist "get-away" place that travel guides call "magical."

Labrador Today

Many more settlers came to Labrador when the natural resources developments began in the 1940s and 1950s. Although Labrador's area is over twice that of the island of Newfoundland, it has only nine percent of the province's population.

Iron ore mines had been developed in western Labrador in the 1950s and settlements grew in Labrador City and nearby Schefferville, Québec. The only way in or out of these northern areas was by plane. However, in 1954 the Québec North Shore and Labrador Railway became an option. This made the development of the huge Churchill Falls Project possible. It became the largest civil engineering project ever undertaken in North America. *(In the 1970's, our friends living in Schefferville, Québec would put their car on a freight train flat deck and send it down to Sept-Iles on the coast of Québec where we lived. In winter, we would park it in our yard and plug the engine into a heater. Our friends would arrive by passenger train a few days later, unplug the heater and drive out to Québec City. The winters were so cold, we had to plug the cars in to keep the battery warm or they would not start.)*

You might associate the name Labrador with the family-friendly dog, the Labrador retriever. They are commonly used as guide dogs for people with disabilities. Law enforcement officers use them to detect narcotics and as search and rescue dogs.

Labrador Retrievers – black, yellow and chocolate brown
(Don't you just want to take one home with you…but which one?)

Did you know …

* On Signal Hill in St. John's, Marconi received the first wireless transatlantic transmission from Wexford County, Britain, on Dec. 12, 1901. *(I wonder what he would think of today's cell phones…)*

* Labrador in winter is a land of tundra, ice and barren rock. The temperature can be "bone chilling." The average July temperatures reach only to about 13 °C and they also drop as low as -51 °C. The island's temperature is much more pleasant. *(I chose summer as the best time to visit!)*

* The huge Newfoundland dog is a master at long-distance swimming and has true lifesaving instincts in the water. The dog is large enough to bring drowning victims ashore. These dogs are known for their giant size, intelligence, tremendous strength, calm dispositions, and loyalty. *(I know they have huge appetites, too!)*

The huge and loveable Newfoundland dog

* USA's 15th President, James Buchanan's large Newfoundland dog, "Lara," was a celebrity around the White House. She would lay motionless for hours with one eye opened and one eye closed, always sure to keep an eye on her owner.

*In 1959, the Hibernia oil fields were discovered off the coast of Newfoundland and Labrador. The Hibernia "platform" was towed to the oil field and set on the ocean floor in June 1997. The oil began to flow in November. The platform is 224 m high. This is half the height of New York's Empire State Building and about 33 m taller than the Calgary Tower. It holds five modules for drilling and pumping the oil and a utilities module for generators and equipment. One module is for living accommodations for the 185 people who work on the platform. *(I'm happy just to look at it through binoculars, thanks!)*

The Hibernia platform was built to withstand a collision with a one million tonne iceberg. *(Do you think that might make it safer than the "unsinkable" Titanic?)*

* The Royal National Mission to Deep Sea Fishermen sent Wilfred Grenfell, MD, to Newfoundland in 1892 to improve the plight of coastal residents and fishermen. He was knighted in 1927 for his medical, educational and social work. You can visit Sir Wilfred Grenfell's house in St. Anthony as it is now a museum. Learn more about Dr. Grenfell in Newfoundland here: Grenfell-properties.com/about_dr.grenfell.php

* One of the most delicious berries found in Newfoundland is the bakeapple. No kidding, bakeapples are *berries* and it takes hours to find enough to fill a cup! But they make scrumptious jam. Salmon berries are pretty yummy too! *(And they're easier to pick!)*

* If you are up the coast near St. Anthony in late summer, you can watch the amazing sight of capelin swarming into shore. These small, silvery fish (similar to freshwater smelt) provide a vital link in the food chain between plankton and larger animals.

* Whale watching is a must for tourists and the Bay of Bulls is the place to go – and be sure to watch for the colourful puffins on the rocks! *(I love their brightly coloured beaks! Have you ever seen any?)*

* In 1932, Amelia Earhart was the first woman to complete a transatlantic solo flight. She took off from Harbour Grace, Newfoundland, and landed safely in Northern Ireland. Unfortunately, in 1937, her plane disappeared in the Pacific Ocean and has never been found.

* Over the years, the women of Newfoundland have become famous for their crafts, especially their wool sweaters, mitts and scarves with distinctive patterns – like these snowflake mittens. *(I found the craft shops across the province full of the beautiful handiwork of the women of Newfoundland and Labrador. I loved seeing a person's work displayed in a wee porch or verandah of the artist's home, always with a little "welcome" sign and an invitation to "stop by.")*

These colourful examples of handiwork can be found in the NONIA store in St. John's. See more in the Resource Page.

Handcrafted by the women of Newfoundland and Labrador *(Photo by NONIA)*

3

The Maritimes – Canada's three seaside provinces

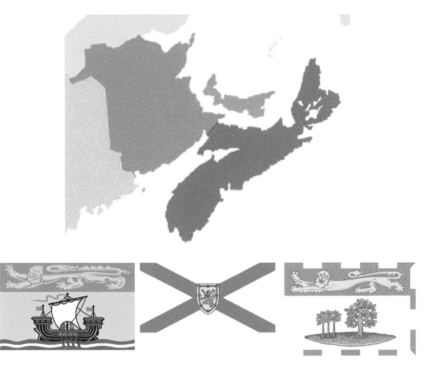

Population: 2,813,102 (2011)

The word maritime means "of the sea," so these three provinces on the eastern seaboard of Canada are considered Maritime Provinces. All territories and provinces of Canada, except Alberta and Saskatchewan, border the sea. In Canada, the term "Maritimes" has always been collectively applied to New Brunswick, Nova Scotia, and Prince Edward Island, all of which snuggle into the Atlantic Ocean on Canada's east coast.

Compared to the other provinces and territories, each of the Maritime Provinces is quite small. Altogether they cover only about 1% of Canada's land surface. Their combined population is around 1,900,000 people. Compare that to over two million people in the *city* of Toronto, Ontario, then think of where you'd want to be in rush hour traffic! *(I'll take Moncton, Halifax or Charlottetown any day!)*

The sea dominates these provinces with jagged coastlines, beautiful bays, sandy beaches and towering cliffs. They have some of the prettiest towns in Canada and the freshest tasting lobster in the world. *(Absolutely! No exaggeration at all!)*

You'll learn more details about each of these provinces in the next three chapters.

History

Thousands of years before the white explorers arrived in the 16th and 17th centuries, this maritime area was home to the Mi'kmaq and Maliseet Aboriginal groups. The influence of the Atlantic Ocean greatly shaped their lifestyle and they adapted to its effects over time. Agricultural conditions were poor due to the harsh climates and these groups became masters of fishing, hunting and managing the natural resources. These First Nations communities have distinct and stimulating cultures, traditions and history.

A cheerful Mi'Kmaq Drummer

The ocean was crucial to the development of the Maritimes. Over the last 300 years it brought waves of fishermen, whalers and settlers from Europe. Early in the 1600s, the French arrived and French Acadia gradually came into existence. Scattered settlements were united with a common language, culture and economy. *(Parlez-vous Français?)*

Boundaries, at that time, were unclear, and in 1621 the Scots claimed this territory, naming it Nova Scotia. In the 1700s, the Maritimes were at the heart of the epic struggle between Britain and France for North America. Settlers were ruled by France, and then Britain until *finally*, in 1713, Acadia changed hands for the last time and became an English possession. The Acadians tried to say they were "neutral" in the fights between France and Britain. They also attempted to convince both countries that Acadian identity was unique.

In 1755, however, the English felt these French-speaking Acadians were not *really* as neutral as they said they were. They were considered a threat to the security of the British cause. The British solution was to expel these settlers from their land. Between 1755 and 1763 over three quarters of the Acadian population were deported - to France, the Annapolis Valley in Nova Scotia and to Maryland, USA. Some journeyed back from France to Louisiana, USA, and some of their travels formed the basis of the long poem *Evangeline* by Longfellow. By 1800 there were about 8,000 Acadians living in the Maritimes. *(More about the expulsion of the Acadians will be coming in the New Brunswick chapter. I love reading their fascinating history but am saddened to learn about their expulsion from the land their forefathers had settled for so many years.)*

In the 1800s, to have greater political power, the three Maritime Provinces were going to unite. But in 1867, the big push began to form the Dominion of Canada. New Brunswick and Nova Scotia joined Québec and Ontario to form the new country of Canada, but PEI said "No thanks. We're fine as we are." *(They really wanted to be independent, eh?)*

Now that Canada had become a country within the "British Empire," a great mixture of nationalities came into the region – Scots, Irish, German and Swiss. The hundreds of thousands of European immigrants arriving in Canada in the 1900s did not change this basic Anglo-Saxon and Acadian ethnic mix. This was because so many immigrants bypassed the Maritimes and flooded into central Canada. *(Those immigrants didn't know what a wonderful Maritime lifestyle they had missed having.)*

The Maritimes Today

Today, the descendants of the Acadians (called "Cajuns") keep the Acadian culture alive and well, not only in New Brunswick, but also in Louisiana, USA. It is their songs that have influenced American popular music for many decades, especially country music. You can find some on YouTube – even some with great pictures of New Brunswick moose! *(Moose is both the singular and plural form of the word so "mooses" isn't really a word.)* See more here: youtube.com/watch?v=vmtjkgDs0w0

Many people in New Brunswick continue to affirm their Acadian distinctiveness. They find ways to show "Acadian" present reality as well as an eventful past. The Maritime Provinces boast a rich legacy of historic sites, many associated with the French-speaking Acadians. The following three chapters will explain more.

The Atlantic Ocean also accounted for the Maritimes' greatest industries of ship building and fishing. They continue to contribute to this area's present day economy. Forestry is also important, especially in New Brunswick, where trees cover 84% of the province.

Since becoming a nation in 1867, it seems Canada began to stress unlimited size and to focus on developing the west. This has left Maritimers feeling left out of Canada's development. These days, tourism has become the mainstay of the Maritimes. This is a thanks in part to the book *Anne of Green Gables* set in Prince Edward Island and the ship with the tall masts, the Bluenose II built in Nova Scotia. Tourists are drawn to the strong Acadian culture so evident in New Brunswick.

New Brunswick, Nova Scotia and Prince Edward Island are on Atlantic Standard (Daylight) Time. When entering New Brunswick from Maine, USA or the province of Québec, your watch should be set *ahead* one hour. If you continue on to Newfoundland and Labrador, add another half hour to your watch! *(The residents of this province like to be unique, eh?)*

Did you know ...

* L. M. Montgomery, born in Prince Edward Island in 1874, wrote a whole series of "Anne" books that followed *Anne of Green Gables*. She also wrote several other series of books still loved - especially by young girls - even though they were published almost 100 years ago!

* Mary Pratt, born in Fredericton, New Brunswick, is a Canadian painter. She has a realist style and first produced still life paintings. Two of them were featured on Canadian 2007 postage stamps. She still lives in Newfoundland and continues to paint and write. She has been awarded nine honorary degrees from various universities in Canada.

B.C. Delicious by Mary Pratt *(Equinox Gallery, Vancouver, BC)*

* Bliss Carman is a beloved poet of New Brunswick. *(I especially like his poem Vestigia.)* He loved writing both prose and poetry about the Maritimes. Imagine! He and I graduated from the University of New Brunswick – although not at the same time*! (He earned his MA in 1884 & I received my Bachelor of Nursing in 1968, but I felt certain that his spirit was alive and well on the beautiful UNB campus!)*

* Prince Edward Island hosted the Charlottetown Conference in 1864, which began the process of forming the Confederation of Canada. BUT PEI was considering staying a British colony, becoming its own country or joining the United States as its northernmost state! Finally, in 1873, *six years after confederation*, Prime Minister John A. Macdonald bribed

PEI into joining Canada by paying off its extensive railroad construction debts! *(PEI joined Canada v e r y reluctantly, but I think now they are happy they did!)*

* When you visit the Maritimes, you'll find friendly people who enjoy a slower pace of life and who will give you a warm welcome. Maritimers seem very "laid back" and not in such a rush as those who live in Québec and Ontario. *(Not only my opinion! I bet you'll agree when you visit!)*

* In some Canadian provinces, you can purchase individual cans of beer. I have read that in Newfoundland and New Brunswick it's different. It is apparently a law that the smallest unit of beer that can be sold in liquor stores is a six-pack. *(Seems a good excuse to shop with friends!)*

* Over the years, the Maritimes has had some 'weird' laws. In Yarmouth, Nova Scotia, about 90 years ago, there was a law for pedestrians. Just like vehicles on the road, people had to pass oncoming pedestrians to the right. Also, it was absolutely against the law for two or more baby carriages to be wheeled side by side on any sidewalk! *(I wonder what the fine was!)*

* In the 1800s in Summerside, Prince Edward Island, if you were moving a house and you had to rest for a while, you couldn't just leave it "unattended." It was against the law to leave it "stand on a street or square without someone watching it." *(Gives a new meaning to the phrase "house sitting"! That's the phrase we use when someone stays in our house while we are away.)*

* In Scotland, the "tartan" was a great source of pride and was worn by the Scots to identify the various clans or families. Scottish settlers first brought the tartans to Canada. Now, all of Canada's provinces and territories, except Nunavut, have regional tartans. Nova Scotia was the first to adopt a regional tartan in 1956. *(I love the blue colour.)*

**The beautiful colours of
the Nova Scotia Tartan**

**All of Canada's
Regional Tartans**

You may see all the tartans of Canada if you put this address into your browser:

en.wikipedia.org/wiki/Regional_tartans_of_Canada

* Fiddleheads are a Maritime delicacy you have to try. They are sprouts of the ostrich fern that are gathered in early spring for eating. *(Délicieuse!)*

**New Brunswick fiddleheads – ready to
steam and eat!** *(Photo: Niamh Shields)*

New Brunswick Provincial Flower

Purple Violet
Jane Crosby, 2014, watercolour 21 x 16 cm

4

New Brunswick (NB) – Canada's only_____

Read on to find out

Gulf of St Lawrence
Golfe du Saint-Laurent

PRINCE EDWARD ISLAND
ILE-DU-PRINCE-EDOUARD

Population: 751,171 (2011)   Joined Confederation: July 1, 1867

Main Cities: Bathurst, Campbellton, Chatham, Dalhousie, Edmundston, Fredericton (capital), Moncton, Saint John ("Saint" is always spelled out), Woodstock

Places to Visit/Things to See:

Magnetic Hill	Reversing Falls	Beaverbrook Art Gallery
Shediac	Hopewell Rocks	King's Landing Historical Settlement

New Brunswick (**NB**) is unique - it is Canada's only official bilingual province with about 33% of the population being francophone. Most are of Acadian origin. NB is the largest of the three Maritime Provinces. It was created when the British Colony of Nova Scotia was divided in 1784. Saint John is the most populous city but its capital is Fredericton. *(Where I* *spent 4 great years at the University of New Brunswick - UNB. The campus was beautiful and overlooked the St. John River.)*

Possibly the oldest province in Canada, New Brunswick is located under the province of Québec's Gaspé Peninsula and beside the State of Maine in the USA. It has a beautiful seacoast and Prince Edward Island and Nova Scotia shelter it from the Atlantic Ocean so its temperature varies with the seasons.

History

Long before any European settlers arrived, the Mi'kmaq Aboriginal tribe occupied the land in eastern NB and the Maliseet tribe lived mostly in the Saint John River Valley. The Passamaquoddy tribe was situated in the southwest, around Passamaquoddy Bay. The Aboriginal tribes crisscrossed the land depending on the season. They hunted and fished and eventually began to trade with the new European settlers. [See the Resources Page for some sites where you can explore more about the Aboriginal/First Nations culture.]

In 1534, Jacques Cartier "sailed through" the area and claimed the land for France but he did not stay. In 1604, Samuel de Champlain and Pierre Duga arrived. They were sent by the King of France to explore and settle the region. By winter's end, they had lost 36 out of 87 members in their party to scurvy. When they moved into the area of Nova Scotia region, they named the whole Atlantic region "Acadie." *(Pronounced A – ca – dee in French and A-cay-di-a in English.)*

The Acadian settlers were caught in the struggle between the French and the British over control of the Atlantic region. Many battles took place during this power struggle. By 1760, France had lost control of all of its North American territories. *(C'etait terrible!)*

Battles in the Maritimes during the American Revolutionary War had a direct effect on the New Brunswick region. The region's population didn't grow until after the Revolution. That's when Britain gave free land to refugee Loyalists from the New England colonies to settle in the area. Apparently, some of the earlier American settlers in New Brunswick actually thought NB should join the New England colonists' cause! (i.e. to boycott a tax the British put on tea) *(That means there could have been some "Canadians" at the "Boston Tea Party"!)* See more about this era here:

history.com/topics/american-revolution/american-revolution-history

Some of the Acadians deported from Nova Scotia, found their way back to "Acadie" during the late 18th and early 19th centuries. They settled mostly in coastal regions of the new colony of New Brunswick and tried to maintain their language and traditions.

Immigration in the early part of the 19th century was mostly from the west of Britain, and from Scotland and Ireland. Often, the Irish had first lived in Newfoundland before moving on to New Brunswick.

Throughout the 19th century, shipbuilding became the dominant industry. Resource-based industries such as logging and farming were also important. From the 1850s, through to the end of the century, several railways were built across the province. They made it easier for the inland resources to make it to markets elsewhere. In the 20th century, small numbers of eastern European, Dutch, German, Italian and South and East Asian immigrants settled in the larger cities in New Brunswick.

New Brunswick Today

New Brunswick is one of the most densely forested regions in the world. Forests cover about 84% of the province and the forestry industry definitely boosts its economy. Spruce, fir, and tamarack are most common, also maple, birch and pine. *(I missed the red maple trees when I first moved west. The rich, red colour of maple and sumac leaves, make the changing colours of the leaves in the fall absolutely spectacular. That's a good reason to visit New Brunswick in early October.)*

The rolling hills and spectacular valleys, as well as its historic and modern architecture found in many of its cities, towns and villages offer a wide range of attractions to New Brunswick visitors and residents alike. The tides of the Bay of Fundy – the highest and wildest in the world – have carved a spectacular coastline. The eastern coast is dotted with warm, sandy beaches, featuring the warmest salt water on Canada's east coast. *(Being on Shediac Beach is my best summer memory.)*

Wood product manufacturing, pulp and paper products and professional, scientific and technical services continue to contribute to New Brunswick's economy. The unemployment rate is high, as people seek opportunities farther west in Canada. There has been, however, a small stream of immigrants into the province to offset the numbers who are leaving.

This lighthouse, painted in the colours of the Acadian flag, is a tourist information centre. © Pierre Forgues | Dreamstime.com

Did you know ...

* New Brunswick is home to the longest covered bridge in the world. Opened in 1901 in Hartland, it began a tradition! It was **the** place where local couples stopped their carriages to share a kiss. *(I guess they don't stop cars there for a kiss these days...but we did once when we were driving through!)*

The Hartland Bridge, Hartland, New Brunswick

* The Reversing Falls in Saint John are amazing! They flow in opposite directions - at the same time. Apparently this effect is caused by tidal action originating in the Southern Indian Ocean! This site on the Internet will give you more information on these tides:

   tourismnewbrunswick.ca

* You probably know the film "Moguls" Metro-Goldwyn-Meyer and Warner Bros. It is interesting that Louis B. Meyer was the son of a junk dealer in Saint John, New Brunswick and Jack L. Warner was a native of London, Ontario. *(I didn't know that! Amazing the things we don't learn in school!)*

* The range between low and high tide in the Bay of Fundy is the biggest in the world at 14 meters. *(No exaggeration!)*

* The fastest clipper ship ever built was built in Saint John, NB, in 1851. The *Marco Polo* broke the round trip speed record between Liverpool, UK and Australia. The record had been six months but this chipper clipper did it in five months and 21 days!

In 1999, Canada and Australia jointly released commemorative stamps... featuring MARCO POLO. The Canadian stamp shows the ship passing Partridge Island as it left Saint John. The Australian 85c stamp was one of a series that celebrated famous colonial clipper ships. The Aussies... embraced the story of the MARCO POLO for her role in delivering emigrant families and Gold Rush hopefuls to the colony, quickly and safely.

* The Petitcodiac River has a unique tidal bore. A few young men made history in 2013 by riding this "longest wave." You can see their feat on YouTube!

* Many New Brunswick place names – cities, rivers, etc. – are Aboriginal or Acadian names. How many can you pronounce?

Bouctouche, Kennebecasis, Kouchibouguac, Memramcook, Miramichi, Passamaquoddy, Restigouche, Richibucto, and Sackville. *(Ok, that last one was easy! But can you imagine learning to spell all these places? I think even Spell Check gets some of them wrong!)*

* The Acadian Peninsula in northeast New Brunswick is the largest producer of peat moss in Canada, and the second largest producer in the world.

* Fredericton has a wonderful Art Gallery. It is the home of the **huge** painting of the prominent Spanish surrealist painter, Salvador Dali, called "Santiago El Grande." *(It's awesome!)* You just have to check it out on the Internet. You can find it here: dali.com/blog/santiago-el-grande *(I had not seen the painting since studying at the University in Fredericton. Last year, when in Florida, USA, we toured the Salvador Dali museum in St. Petersburg. Imagine how astonished we were when we walked around a corner and there was the huge Santiago El Grande painting! Just then, the tour guide said we were very fortunate to see it because it was on loan from the Art Gallery in Fredericton, New Brunswick and was supposed to have been sent back yesterday! We were as awed by the painting that day as we had been the first time we had seen it 47 years before in NB! I think you'll be awed too.)*

* A knit cap worn all over Canada is called a "toque". Originally made of wool, and narrowing at the top, many variations exist. This kind of cap was a common form of headgear for fishers, hunters and others working outdoors. It is found all over the world under many local names.

**Like an original one (left) and one
of many varieties made today**

* Just east of Moncton is a lovely seaside town of Shediac where you can taste the best fried clams in the world. *(Well...ok, I might be exaggerating a bit. Honestly, though, I enjoyed them for all the years I lived in Moncton and have yet to find any as tasty. Have you found a great place for tasty fried clams?)*

* Shediac also has the best and tastiest Atlantic lobsters *ever* but you have to be there in lobster season so be sure to go in late July and August. *(The lobster roll is my fave! Delicious!)* Lobsters can be small or large, but not as large as the one greeting you as you enter Shediac! The lobster sculpture is 10.7 m long by 4.9 m high and weighs 90 tonnes.

* The Hopewell Rocks are amazing shapes caused by tidal erosion. They are about 12-21 m tall and are also called the Flowerpot Rocks. The base of these formations is covered in water twice a day. It's best to check the tide table before taking the short drive from Moncton to see these natural "Flowerpots." The high tide can be as high as 16 metres.

The Rocks at low tide   **The Rocks at rising tide**

Nova Scotia Provincial Flower

Mayflower
Jane Crosby, 2014, watercolour 14 x 13 cm

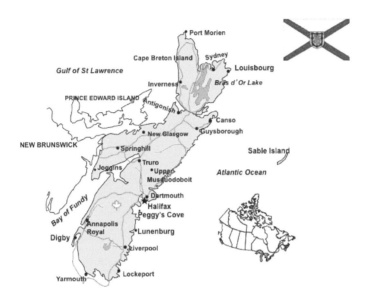

Nova Scotia (NS) – Canada's Ocean Playground

<u>Population</u>: 945,061 (2012)   <u>Joined Confederation</u>: July1, 1867

<u>Main Cities</u>: Amherst, Dartmouth, Halifax (Capital), New Glasgow, Pictou, Sydney, Truro

<u>Places to Visit/Things to See</u>:

Citadel Hill & Fort George, Halifax	Peggy's Cove
Fortress Louisbourg – Cape Breton	The Cabot Trail, Cape Breton
Bluenose II, Lunenberg	The Miners Museum, Cape Breton
Joggins Fossil Cliffs – UNESCO world Natural Heritage Site	

The south shores of Nova Scotia and Cape Breton are washed by the Atlantic Ocean and provide a "playground" for boating, swimming and fishing.

History

The Mi'kmaq First Nations people had inhabited the land in Nova Scotia for centuries. With a climate that wasn't suitable for agriculture, the small semi-nomadic bands subsisted by fishing and hunting. The moose was the most important animal used for food, clothing and tools. They were very skilled with the bow and arrow and also hunted deer, caribou, bear and small animals. Porcupine quills were used in decorative beadwork done by women. They ate a variety of fish, such as salmon, lobster, and squid. *(I would definitely not have wanted to collect the porcupine quills! Would you?)*

The Mi'kmaq territory was the first part of North America where Europeans came to take resources from the sea. European fishermen and whalers in the early part of the 16th century salted their fish on their way home. Later, they began to set up camps on shore to dry the cod as the Mi'kmaq did. These camps would then trade with the Mi'kmaq fishermen and the trading began to include furs.

There were many French-English "skirmishes" in the mid 1600s and at one point Nova Scotia actually became a Scottish colony! The French established the Fortress of Louisbourg on Cape Breton Island in 1713. It was enormous and took 3 decades to build. It was costing so much that the French king joked he expected to see the fort from his palace in France! Today, Fort Louisbourg is a National Historic Site showing how people lived in the 18th century. You can see more on the Internet here:

novascotia.com

Sambro Island Lighthouse near Halifax, NS. Oldest lighthouse in North America (1758). *(Photo courtesy of Paul Illsley)*

Nova Scotia has the largest number of lighthouses of any province in Canada. They have guided mariners to safety for hundreds of years. Although they have been replaced by modern technology, each lighthouse remains an important symbol of the past and of the picturesque coastal landscape.

In the 1700s, shiploads of Scots, who were forced off their ancestral lands in Scotland, came to St. John's Island. This small island, just off the east coast of both New Brunswick and Nova Scotia, was considered part of Nova Scotia. However, in 1769 it became a separate colony called **Prince Edward Island**.

The Scottish immigrants brought their love of the tartan cloth with them. Clan tartans gave way to district tartans. They reflected geographical areas and linked land and community through symbolic and imaginative use of colour. *(The Scots couldn't do without their tartans!)*

The Nova Scotia Tartan is a predominantly light blue and blue tartan with green and white. It's made into everything from kilts to baby's bibs and from bow ties to purses.

Just as the Scots must have their tartans, they must also have their beloved Highland Games. The Highland Games in Antigonish, Nova Scotia, are the longest running Highland Games in North America. They have been held yearly since 1863! Great bagpipe band competitions are also usually held at the games. You may hear different "pipe bands" on youtube videos. *(But to really experience the music of Scotland, you have to attend a tattoo. This is a musical event with many marching bands playing hundreds of bagpipes at once. The one I experienced in Halifax made my "Scottish genes" absolutely tingle!)*

In the 1800s, many immigrants decided to leave Nova Scotia because of the hardships they faced. In the 1850s, Reverend Norman McLeod led a shipload of about 800 Scottish residents from St. Ann's, Nova Scotia, to Waipu, New Zealand. *(When in New Zealand a few years ago, I found a small museum in Waipu about this group and its journey from NS to NZ. I had never heard of it before! Their descendants now number in the ten thousands! Maybe you have some ancestors in New Zealand!)*

Nova Scotia Today

Traditionally, Nova Scotia has relied on its natural resources but changes have been needed in recent years. The fish stocks have declined and coal mining has virtually ceased. Today, the Nova Scotia wine industry has become the third most recognized wine region in Canada. By 2020 the province hopes to see 20 wineries established. This is no small feat for the second smallest province in Canada! *(I'm not sure they will catch up to the well-established British Columbia and Ontario wines very soon!)*

Agriculture has grown in importance, especially in the Annapolis Valley area. Some of Canada's best apples come from Nova Scotia. This small province is also the world's largest exporter of Christmas trees and lobster! *(I never knew that!)*

From the cruise ships that arrive in the Port of Halifax, to the tourists who explore its culture and historical places, tourism provides a major economic boost for Nova Scotia. Golf lovers come to play on some of the best courses in Canada. One of the most popular tourist towns is Lunenberg, a UNESCO World Heritage Site – and the birthplace of the famous tall ship the *Bluenose*. You can learn about this amazing racing ship on the Internet here: bluenose.novascotia.ca

Nova Scotia has a growing Information and Technology sector with 500 companies; many institutions for Fine Arts; a thriving music industry, and the tremendous contributions of filmmaking and television. *(I think Nova Scotia is a happenin' place!)*

The Bluenose II – replica of the amazing racing ship Bluenose I and now a NS icon!

Did you know ...

* The movies *Titanic,* (starring Leonardo DiCaprio and Kate Winslet) and *Bowling for Columbine* (with Michael Moore) were both made in Nova Scotia.

* The original *Bluenose* was built to race for the International Fisherman's Trophy in 1921 and was undefeated for **17 years**! The *Bluenose II,* built in Lunenberg in 1963, is an identical replica of the first ship. It has a sailing schedule from June 1st to September 30th each year. But you can go aboard for a tour when she's in her homeport. *(The Bluenose II picture is on the Canadian ten-cent coin. You might want to check out what happened to the* Bluenose I.*)* Learn more here:

thecanadianencyclopedia.ca/en/article/bluenose/

* With its distinctive star shape, the Halifax Citadel is a must to visit! Can you imagine soldiers firing muskets from every angle and large canons booming from its ramparts? *(But this citadel was never attacked!)* Today you will see guards in full uniform and bearskin hats, others in period costume, and men in kilts playing bagpipes.

* Over the years, many movie stars have owned homes in NS, including Jack Nicholson, Billy Joel, Roger Moore and Alan Arkin. (These were probably bought for *"quiet "get-a-ways."*) Donald Sutherland *(MASH, Ordinary People)* spent most of his youth in this province.

* The Halifax Explosion in Dec. 1917 was the largest man-made explosion prior to the development of nuclear weapons. A French cargo ship, fully loaded with wartime explosives, collided with another ship in Halifax Harbour. You can read more about it on the Internet here:

> thecanadianencyclopedia.ca/en/article/halifax-explosion/

You may also see an interesting video here:

> youtube.com/watch?v=cJSta2LPi2Y

* **Anne Murray** is one of Canada's famous songsters. Born in Springhill, NS, her first hit was "Snow Bird." It became the first Gold record <u>ever</u> by a Canadian solo female artist. Do you know it? You can hear Anne sing it on YouTube across the years from the 1970s to the year 2008 when she retired after selling over 54 million records. *(We were at the University of New Brunswick together and I told her one day she would become famous. I loved being right about that!)* ☺

* **"We have struck iceberg   sinking fast   come to our assistance"** was the distress call from the RMS Titanic on April 14, 1912. The "unsinkable" ship sank 3 hours later. The Cunard Liner RMS *Carpathia* rescued over 700 survivors. Four Canadian vessels were sent to carry out the grim task of recovering the bodies. Of the 300 bodies recovered, 100 victims were laid to rest in Halifax cemeteries. *(The Maritime Museum of the Atlantic in Halifax has a permanent display of artifacts from the ill-fated Titanic. You may see them online here:* novascotia.ca/titanic/ *or, better still, spend a few hours browsing the museum in person when you are in Halifax. It's really fascinating!)*

* During WW I, Halifax became a busy international port and naval facility. The harbour served as a major shipment point for war supplies and troop ships to Europe. It was also a receiving point for hospital ships returning the wounded. The port of Halifax is always ice-free and it is also a day's sailing time closer to Europe than from the American coast.

* The Cape Breton Miners Museum pays tribute to the region's "long and rich history of coal mining." It's also home to *Men of the Deeps*, a choir of working and retired Cape Breton miners. It was formed in 1966 to preserve in song some of the rich folklore of those who worked thousands of feet underground. This group has travelled around the world and has been recognized as a special Canadian ambassador. You can hear them here: menofthedeeps.com/videos-2/

* More tourists visit Peggy's Cove than almost any other part of Nova Scotia. This once quiet fishing village, a short drive from Halifax, has a famous lighthouse (1915), salty sea air and the remarkable roar of the Atlantic waves crashing against the rocks. *(Running over these rocks was always – for me - a thrill of summers spent in NS! I could also mail postcards in the tiny post office that used to be in the lighthouse. Do you remember a favourite place from your childhood?)*

The Lighthouse (1915) at Peggy's Cove

Prince Edward Island Provincial Flower

Lady's Slipper
Jane Crosby, 2014, watercolour 26 x 19 cm

6

Prince Edward Island (PEI) – Home
of *Anne of Green Gables*

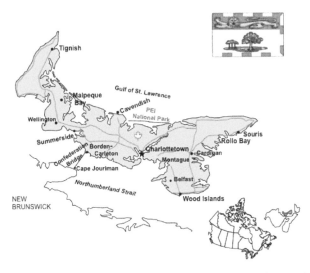

Population: 145,855 (2011)   Joined Confederation: July 1, 1873

Cities: Charlottetown (Capital), Summerside

Towns: Afton, Alberton, Cornwall, Kensington, Montague, Souris, Stratford

Places to Visit/Things to See:

Play golf on one of 33 courses   Join Confederation Players Walking Tours
Anne of Green Gables Home   Rollo Bay Fiddle Festival

Affectionately know as "PEI," this is Canada's smallest province - 224 km long and from six to 64 km wide. There is no place on the island that is more than 16 kilometers from the sea. It is separated from New Brunswick and Nova Scotia by the Northumberland Strait.

England's Queen Victoria's father was Prince Edward and the island was named in honour of him. It is often called "the Garden Province" because half the land is cultivated. Charlottetown takes its name from Queen Charlotte, the wife of England's King George III. It is the largest city with an estimated population of 62,477.

History

For about 12,000 years, the ancestors of the Mi'kmaq Aboriginal people lived on Prince Edward Island. They were probably following the caribou, and other large land mammals. The Mi'kmaq called the island "Epekwitk" – meaning *land cradled in the waves*. *(Doesn't that make a nice picture?)* They believed that the Great Spirit formed the island by placing dark red clay in the shape of a crescent on the waters. They lived in birch bark wigwams (tepees), which several families would sometimes share. They moved with the seasons, depending where different foods were available. This cycle of land and resource use is still carried out by the Mi'kmaq today. The coming of the Europeans brought many changes to their way of living.

In 1534, Jacques Cartier was the first European to explore the island, then known as Île St-Jean (Island of Saint John). There was no permanent settlement for about the next 200 years. In 1719, a French colony was formed and the French considered the Mi'kmaq their friends. Joint celebrations were held, and the Mi'kmaq traded furs for many things that made their lives easier. They could now use cooking pots and iron knives instead of flaked stone tools. However, the trade of furs for alcohol made life a lot harder for the Mi'kmaq people. They continued to help the Acadian (French) settlers to produce enough food to survive.

In 1758, when the British captured the Fortress of Louisbourg and gained control of the Island of Saint John, they expelled the French farmers. (The same way they had expelled the Acadians in New Brunswick three years previously). Without consulting either the farmers or the Mi'kmaq, the British divided the land into large lots and gave them to British citizens. Loyalists, people living in the American colonies who remained loyal to the King of England, joined the British settlers in the 1780s.

In the early 1800s in northern Scotland, the "Clearances" occurred. "Crofters" (farmers) were forced off their land so sheep could be raised. In 1803, Lord Selkirk envisioned these farmers forming agricultural communities in British North America (i.e. soon-to-be-Canada). He transported shiploads of Scottish groups to Prince Edward Island and planted the colony in the southeastern part of the province. This Belfast area quickly became a village. Between 1845 and 1852, displaced Irish potato famine refugees joined the Scots. Prince Edward Island became the 7th Canadian province in 1873 – six years after Canada was created. There's an interesting reason for the wait to join. *(You can find it if you go back and check out Chapter 3 – The Maritimes. It was mentioned there.)*

Prince Edward Island didn't think the terms for joining Canada were very favourable to the island. In 1867, they chose to remain part of the nation of Great Britain and Ireland. They began to examine various options. One was to become a distinct dominion unto itself. Another was to take the offer from USA delegations to join the United States of America! *(I am certainly glad they did not decide to take that option!)*

In 1871, the colony began constructing a railway and began negotiations with the United States. In 1873, Prime Minister Sir John A. Macdonald, anxious to stop any American expansion into Canada, negotiated for Prince Edward Island to join Canada. The Federal Government of Canada assumed the colony's extensive railway debts and agreed to a "few other conditions." Prince Edward Island entered Confederation on July 1, 1873. *(Whew! Finally!)*

PEI Today

The population is now about 145,000 – over 75% being of Scottish, Irish and English descent. Only about 15% are of French origin. About 46% of the population lives in a city or town, and the rest of the population live in a rural setting.

The soil in PEI is distinctive red-coloured sandstone and the beaches are fine reddish sand. The soil gets its colour from the high iron content that oxidizes when exposed to the air. There are over 90 sandy beaches on the island! *(This is definitely the place to go swimming!)* After a swim, you might enjoy a stroll along the floating Boardwalk to see the Greenwich Dunes in Prince Edward Island National Park. See more here:

pnipe.peinp@pc.gc.ca

**The Boardwalk in the Greenwich Section of
Prince Edward Island National Park**

Lobster season happens twice a year in Prince Edward Island but in different parts of the province. The first season runs from May 1st until the end of June, and the second from mid-August to mid-October. *(Choose your best time to enjoy a yummy lobster feast - with lots of melted butter for dipping!)*

When travelling in Prince Edward Island, as well as lobster, you may sample delicious tuna, cod, and mackerel. Also try the excellent oysters that are harvested for Canada and exported throughout the world.

Food processing is an important industry (bottling, canning, freezing) and about 30% of Canada's potatoes are grown in PEI. Farmers also grow apples, strawberries, blueberries, carrots, onions, tomatoes and cereal crops.

Prince Edward Island has a mild climate because of the warm waters of the Gulf of St. Lawrence but there are frequent winter storms with an average yearly snowfall of 300 cm (almost 10 feet). Also, it gets very windy on the Island.

Until 1997, Prince Edward Island was cut off from the mainland of New Brunswick and only accessible by ferry. But now there is a huge "Confederation Bridge" joining the two provinces. To travel to Nova Scotia from PEI, however, you still have to take a ferry from Wood Islands, PEI to Caribou, Nova Scotia. It's about a 75-minute trip.

Did you know

* Confederation Bridge between New Brunswick and Prince Edward Island is almost 13 km long and takes about 12 minutes to cross. It is free to travel to the island but you must pay a toll when you are ready to leave.

Much faster than the old ferry, but not as relaxing!

* Charlottetown is the "birthplace of Canada" where leaders met in 1864 to begin to discuss the formation of our country. *(Discussions continued elsewhere for 3 more years!)*

* Harvested for its carrageenan, Irish moss is a specific type of seaweed that's gathered in PEI by pulling a special rake along the rocks or over the sea floor. It is used to thicken ice cream, cheese and toothpaste. In the past, as many as 250 people would harvest the Irish moss when it would wash up on the beach after a bad storm.

Solidly built to withstand the ice that covers this waterway in winter

* Lucy Maud Montgomery is the author of the delightful book *Anne of Green Gables*. In Cavendish, you can visit Green Gables House, a museum about the author. The series of "Anne books" is world famous, and has been translated into 20 languages.

* The Robert Harris Collection of the Confederation Centre of the Arts in Charlottetown consists of some 5,000 works of art. Harris was one of the Group of Seven, a group of well-known Canadian landscape painters from 1920 to 1933.

* Sometimes known as the "Garden of the Gulf," Prince Edward Island has established itself as a North American leader in wind energy. It is leading the way in emerging renewable energies. However, not all PE Islanders believe the wind turbines are as efficient as they are declared to be. *(I remember it was very windy waiting for the ferry to take us from Wood Islands to Nova Scotia. I think it's great PEI can "harness the wind" as an energy source. What do you think about these wind turbines?)*

**Over 30% of PEI's electrical needs are
met through wind development**

* Until May 2008, you could only buy beer and soda (or pop) in Prince Edward Island in glass bottles not in cans or plastic bottles. The "ban the can" legislation was an environmental measure in response to public concerns over litter. Also, glass bottles could be recycled many times. *(Sounded like a good idea to me!)*

* The principal industries of the province are agriculture, tourism and fishing. The processing of frozen fried potatoes, green vegetables, and berries is a leading business activity. The food industry is the most important contributor to the provincial economy. Many people around the world know the best mussels come from PEI! The island has been named the second best "foodie getaway" in the world by Zagat. *(A company that produces restaurant guides for over 100 countries in the world. Isn't this amazing for this little island?)*

* During the last century, there was a large mink and fox fur industry in PEI. When it disbanded, the foxes were set free and became a very common wild animal. One of the golf courses is called Fox Meadows and there are families of foxes that live on the course and steal golf balls. *(I have it on a good PEI resident's authority that this is a true story!)*

* A native of Prince Edward Island, Charles Coghlan, died in Galveston, Texas, USA, in 1899. He was buried in a lead-lined coffin. Less than a year later, a hurricane struck Galveston bringing widespread flooding and washed Coghlan's coffin away. In 1908, off the coast of PEI, fishermen pulled a coffin covered in barnacles from the water. It seems Mr. Coghlan had returned home on the Gulf Stream! *(Quite the story!)*

The wild, colourful lupins are one of the beauties of PEI
(It was fascinating to see these beautiful flowers also growing wild in New Zealand)

Québec Provincial Flower

Blue Flag Iris
Jane Crosby, 2015, watercolour 27 x 14 cm

7

Québec (QC) – La Belle Province

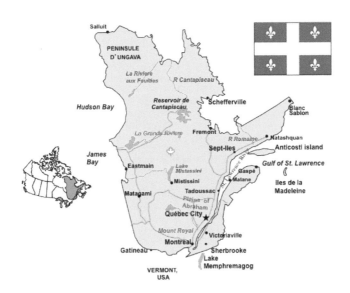

<u>Population</u>: 8,028,400 (2013)   <u>Joined Confederation</u>: July 1, 1867

<u>Main Cities</u>: Québec City (capital), Gatineau, Montréal, Sherbrooke (← *I was born there!* ☺)

<u>Places to Visit/Things to See</u>:

Old Québec – Québec City   Montmorency Falls Park, Québec City
The Québec Citadel   Mount Royal - Montréal
Canadian Museum of History - Gatineau
Plains of Abraham - Québec City

The name Québec comes from an Algonquin word meaning "where the river narrows," referring to the St. Lawrence River. On the map, you can see how narrow the river is at Montréal and Québec City. It gets wider flowing northeast past Sept-Îles, and then it disappears as it flows into the Gulf of St. Lawrence. *(Working in the hospital in Sept- Îles for three years is where I learned to speak French. It was very different from learning French in school!)*

57

History

Evidence suggests that big-animal hunters crossed the Bering Strait from Eurasia into North America over a land and ice bridge (Beringa) that existed about 10,000 years ago. Small isolated groups began migrating south into the interior lands. The precise dates and routes these groups took are still being debated.

The Inuit in the northern parts of Canada are descended from these people groups. Apparently, so are the ten indigenous tribes in present day Québec. The province has a rich and varied history over the centuries as the Aboriginal Peoples created their own languages, cultural pursuits and self-government. It could be seen over the centuries that the European explorers and traders did not understand the natives' culture, their sense of being one with the land and the value they placed on its preservation. The lifestyle of the Aboriginal people began to change with the coming of the Europeans. *(I wonder if we - five centuries later - can really understand and appreciate the significance of this lifestyle change for the 'first Canadians.')*

In 1535, Jacques Cartier planted a cross on the Gaspé Peninsula and claimed the land for France. He sailed up and down the St. Lawrence River many times, visiting the village of Hochelaga, an Iroquoian fortified village where Montréal now stands. *(Remember in Chapter One, I mentioned our country might have been called Hochelaga? I'm so glad they chose Canada instead!)*

The modern province occupies much of the land where French settlers founded the colony of Canada (then called New France) in the 17th and 18th centuries. Québec and the Maritime Provinces are Canada's "old world" areas. They must seem quite "new" to people from Europe whose history goes back hundreds of years farther than Canada's.

One of the interesting historical notes is that Donnacona, the Chief of Stadacona (now Québec City), allowed Jacques Cartier to take his two sons back to France for about eight months. They learned French and returned as interpreters for Cartier. *(Can you imagine the culture shock for these two lads to land in modern French cities of the 1500s?)*

In the 1600s Samuel de Champlain claimed the lands of Acadia and Newfoundland and went on to Québec to establish the colony of

L'Habitation, which became Québec City. In Old Québec today you can still see parts of the fort Champlain built there in 1608. It is a UNESCO World Heritage Site. In the mid 1600s, the population of Québec's settlements began to grow. Schools and hospitals were built and a peace treaty was signed with the Iroquois. In the mid 1700s, early settlers and Aboriginal Peoples had to fight against new diseases and hundreds died from smallpox.

In the chapter on New Brunswick you learned that the British were successful in taking over many areas formerly held by the French. They expelled the Acadians from New Brunswick and went on to capture Fort Louisbourg in 1758. Now the British were finally ready to launch an attack to capture Québec City.

In the battle on the Plains of Abraham in 1759, the British defeated the French (See Chapter One). Centuries later, there is still tension between the French and the English. In 1955, Québec replaced its car license plates' motto *La belle province (the beautiful province)* with *Je me souviens (I remember)*. In that year, the historian M. Wade wrote: "When the French Canadian says 'Je me souviens', he not only remembers the days of New France but also the fact that he belongs to a conquered people." This French/English tension is reflected in today's political arena. A Sovereignty Referendum of 1980, for Québec to leave Canada and become its own country, did not pass. As all Canada held its breath, the second Referendum in 1995 *almost* passed. *(The debate continues but so far the inimitable Québec is thankfully still with us!)*

Cornelius Krieghoff, a Dutch painter who came to live in Québec in the 1800s, became interested in the scenery and scenes of everyday life. You may see what Québec looked like centuries ago by viewing some of his paintings on the Internet. *(Note the Hudson Bay point coat. Can't you just feel the cold, crunchy snow in this painting?)*

A Québec winter scene by Cornelius Krieghoff

Québec Today

Modern Québec provides many natural minerals that contribute to Canada's economy. It provides nearly half the country's supply of iron ore and is the world's leading producer of asbestos.

From polar bears to beavers and snowy owls to woodpeckers, the province is home to a variety of wildlife. The vastly different habitats also provide over 2,500 kinds of flowers.

The old and the new co-exist in Québec. In Québec City tourists arrive in the millions each year to walk the city's cobblestone streets and to experience the old historical sites. They are also drawn to the "joie de vivre" (exuberant enjoyment of life) exhibited in the various lively cultural festivals and celebrations.

Québec City is the only walled city in North America. It has been designated as a World Heritage Site – one of the few cities in the world to have this distinction. Every year it hosts the Québec Winter Carnival. This is two weeks full of ice sculptures and French toe-tapping music, free outdoor banquets and outdoor sport events and, of course, Bonhomme! *(Notice his 'original' red toque!)*

Bonhomme (Snowman) the mascot for Québec Winter Carnival

A Québecker is often known to be open-minded, frank, and a *bon vivant* (one who enjoys social occasions and good food and wine). Québec has a vibrant and distinct culture with an active movie and music scene. Giles Vigneault, the composer of *Mon Pays* (My Country) is well known in Canada; Oscar Peterson was a world-famous jazz musician and Leonard Cohen a world-famous singer, poet and novelist. Both were from Québec. There are hundreds more to pursue in online videos.

Québeckers will very quickly warm up and be open with you if they see you have made the effort to learn their language. They will be especially delighted if you can use some Québec slang or ordinary phrases! Below are four easy (and important) French words to learn. You may learn more here: tripadvisor.com

Bonjour *pronounced* **bon-zhoor***)* = Hello

'Oui *(pronounced* **we***)* = yes' **and** Non *(pronounced **naw***)* = no

Merci *(pronounced* **mair-see***)* = Thank you.

S'il vous plaît *(pronounced* **see-voo-play***)* = Please

(Perhaps you can find a Québecker to teach you more!)

Did you know ...

* If you have seen the blockbuster movie *Titanic,* you have heard Céline Dion from Charlemagne, Québec, singing "My Heart Will Go On." Céline has captured hearts all around the world and has had incredible success in both French and English music markets. She has sold over 100 million albums worldwide. Check out her videos online!

* Early settlers used the St. Lawrence River as one way to get around. They used canoes in summer and sleds in winter. When land was divided, it was always important to have access to the river so farms became very narrow. The St. Lawrence River provides a route to the interior of the country. In its Québec waters you may see many sea mammals, including beluga whales, seals, blue whales and orcas. *(Please don't say "killer whales" – the correct word is orcas.)*

* By 1901, the province had become industrialized and over 50% of the population lived in cities, mostly in the southern part of the province. The province is so large that Germany, France and Spain could easily fit inside its borders. *(I never realized it was that large!)*

* Québec has one of the largest Francophone (French-speaking) communities outside France. It is home to over 90% of Canadians of French origin who cherish their "distinct society" within Canada. *(When you visit, you will see some similarities of Québeckers to the Acadian people of the Maritimes. They are both very animated and "talk" with their hands! They also both love lively French music.)*

* Québec has given the National Hockey League many outstanding players. You may still see many of them playing Saturday nights on television's *Hockey Night in Canada*. It first aired in 1952, and is the longest running sports television show in the world. *(1952...ah, probably before you were born – oui?)*

* The province has over *one million* lakes and rivers and eight of the largest rivers flow north into James Bay and Hudson Bay basin. These rivers and diversions of others, provided for the huge James Bay Hydro Electric project. The project covers an area the size of New York State in USA and is one of the largest hydroelectric systems in the world.

* In Northern Québec, winters can be very long and cold with ice and snow often lasting long past June. Summers are usually hot and the southern cities can be *very* humid. *(I remember the day I arrived in Montréal as a new bride. As I stepped down from the train at 9 a.m., I was hit with a wall of hot, humid air that felt so thick I could hardly breathe! Gasping for air, I whispered to my new husband, "Can we please go home to Moncton? There is no air to breathe here!" No luck leaving. We both had jobs waiting.)*

* Trees are a natural resource of Québec and the province has more forest than any other province in Canada. Some of the trees are used in construction, but the best ones – the maple trees - produce the yummy *sirop d'erable* – maple syrup. *("Pancakes anyone?")* You can see how to make maple syrup here:

purecanadamaple.com/pure-maple-syrup/how-maple-syrup-is-made.

* Pierre Elliott Trudeau, Canada's 15th Prime Minister, was born in Montréal, Québec. He was famous for his youthful energy and his opposition to Québec's wanting to separate from Canada. He was in office during the 1970s and 1980s and his personality dominated Canada's political scene. He even had young people happily voting! *(His son, Justin Trudeau, was elected the 23rd Prime Minister of Canada in the October 2015 federal election. His Liberal Party defeated the Conservative Party that had formed the government for the last nine years. He won over the other three federal parties: the New Democratic Party, the Green Party and the Bloc Québecois. When he chose his Cabinet Ministers for Canada's Parliament in Ottawa, Ontario, Trudeau made history! It was the first time the Canadian Cabinet was composed of equal representation from both men and women! You can learn more on the Internet by searching for Justin Trudeau.)*

* The Canadian Museum of Civilization is located in Gatineau, Québec, across the river from Ottawa, Ontario. It contains more than four million artifacts relating to Canada's fascinating social history. This museum is Canada's most visited museum, with an average 1.2 million visitors each year. *(That is a lot of visitors but the Eaton's Shopping Centre in Toronto has one million visitors **each week!**)* The museum continues to study and interpret history, with an emphasis on the culture and heritage of Canada's many peoples. To learn more, take a quick peek here: thecanadianencyclopedia.ca *(This museum provides an awesome variety of exhibits. The artifacts from the West Coast were*

my favourites. Plan to spend at least half a day strolling through! Then, have lunch on site and keep going!)

* Canadians are very proud of our contribution to the exploration of space. Canada has created the Canadarm to "deploy and capture payloads in space." See more here:

canadianinventors.weebly.com/canadarm.html

We are also proud of our 12 Canadian astronauts and these two in particular. Marc Garneau was the first Canadian in space and is now a Member of the Canadian Parliament. Chris Hadfield is the first Canadian to walk in space. He commanded the International space Station in 2013 and posted awesome pictures taken from the spacecraft on social media. *Did you hear him play the guitar "up there"?* Check him out on YouTube and you can find his books at amazon.com.

The Honourable Dr. Marc Garneau, Minister of Transport, Member of the Canadian Parliament

Commander Chris Hadfield, retired
astronaut, spent 166 days in space

After its final mission on June 1, 2011, the Endeavour lands
at the Kennedy Space Center Shuttle Landing Facility

Ontario Provincial Flower

White Trillium
Jane Crosby, 2016, watercolour 21 x 21 cm

8

Ontario (ON) – The Heartland Province

Population: 12.5 million (2012) Joined Confederation: July 1, 1867

Main Cities: Toronto (Capital), Hamilton, Kingston, London, Mississauga, Ottawa, Sault Ste. Marie, Sudbury, Thunder Bay, Windsor

Places to Visit/Things to See:

Parliament Buildings - Ottawa   Toronto Blue Jays Baseball Game
Stratford Festival - Stratford   Toronto's CN Tower
Upper Canada Village - Morrisburg   Niagara Falls
Canada's Wonderland/Amusement Park - Vaughan

History

Ontario is an Iroquois word meaning "beautiful" or "shining water." This province has the most varied landscape in all of Canada. 10,000 years ago, Aboriginal communities populated the vast lands of Ontario. Algonquian-speaking peoples, including the Cree and Ojibwa, lived in the north. They were mostly hunters and gatherers who moved from place to place in search of food.

Iroquoian-speakers, living in the south, moved less often because they could grow crops and catch fish. They also collected the sap from maple trees to sweeten their food. Their tribes included the Huron Confederacy and the Petun. *(We still get the maple syrup to sweeten our food today basically the same way the Aboriginal tribes did centuries ago. It amazes me to think about that!)*

The Europeans began to arrive in the 17th century. In 1610, Henry Hudson reached Hudson Bay looking for the Northwest Passage, a western route to the Orient. Hudson disappeared when his crew mutinied and cast him adrift in the northern sea. *(Nasty crew!)*

Also in 1610 farther south, Samuel de Champlain first connected with the Hurons in Québec. He was amazed at their large, *palisaded towns and cultivated fields. He made maps and notes of everything he saw. *(A palisade was a fence or wall made from wooden stakes or tree trunks and used to enclose a village for defense. See an example below).*

In 1615 a Roman Catholic Jesuit mission was begun in Ontario. When diseases broke out and many Hurons died, they feared that the missionaries' rituals were witchcraft. They blamed the Jesuits for the deaths and the Iroquois killed five Jesuit fathers. The Jesuits continued to live among the Aboriginals and to serve them for hundreds of years.

The French and the British fought each other for control of Ontario and during this time very few settlers came. The British finally succeeded in taking over the land. When the American Revolution (1776-1783) began, many Americans wanted to remain British subjects so they moved into Canada. By 1785, 6,000 - 10,000 Loyalists had arrived in Ontario. *(There was certainly no shortage of land for them to settle on and to begin farming.)*

Among the Loyalists were English, Scottish, German, Aboriginal Peoples and 3,000 African Americans. The names of these 3,000 black people who had served the King, were kept by British naval officers in a document called the *Book of Negroes*. Unless your name was in this record book you could not escape to Canada. The Canadian author, Lawrence Hill, based his novel *The Book of Negroe*s on this document. *(It's a spellbinding book- a good read that's hard to put down! It has also been made into a six part television miniseries first shown in January 2015. I'm sure it would be in your library.)*

Most settled either along the St. Lawrence River, on the shores of eastern Lake Ontario, or in the Niagara region. For 13 years, Britain granted 200 acres of land to the United Empire Loyalists who were leaving the Colonies after the American Revolution. By 1797, York, (now called Toronto), was named the capital of this settlement. *(Who knew back then that Toronto would become the largest city in Canada? It's really a 'mega city' now!)*

The last time the British and Americans were at war with each other was in the War of 1812. It lasted for two and a half years. The issues were complicated and at the end of the war no land boundaries were changed. The war actually strengthened both Canada and America as independent neighbours. You can read more – and see interesting videos - on the Internet here: history.com/topics/war-of-1812

The Ontario settlers built their communities along the waterways. The water provided their power, irrigation, and transportation. In the 1800s, canals were built that connected Ontario with New York, USA, and provided links from the Great Lakes to the Atlantic Ocean.

The Welland Canal was completed in 1829 to connect Lake Erie and Lake Ontario. It became a key section of the St. Lawrence Seaway that enables ships to bypass Niagara Falls. This canal was a major factor in the growth of Toronto.

In 1904, Toronto had a devastating fire that destroyed 104 buildings and put 5,000 people out of work. At that time, the city only had 20,000 residents. The exact cause of the fire was never known but, as a result of the fire, stricter safety laws were introduced and the city's fire department was expanded. *(It only had one fire truck at that time.)*

Ontario Today

Since the mid 19th century, more than 80% of Ontario's population lives in urban areas. Ontario is the province with the largest population in Canada. It is also the economic centre of this vast country. Its main manufacturing product is the automobile and 90% of its exports go to the United States. Ontario attracts one-tenth of *all* foreign direct investment in North America. *(I think that's sort of a big deal – at least to investors!)*

Over the years, the mining industry has produced about $10 billion worth of minerals. However, since about 2008, mining in northern Ontario has slowly been declining. Agriculture in southern Ontario, with its variety of vegetables, fruit and dairy products, has been a big contributor to the province's economy. While farms are declining in number, the province is attempting to create a renewable-energy economy. *(You'll see a 750 kW wind turbine right in downtown Toronto!)*

The service sector plays a large part in Ontario's economy. This includes a large number of industries such as hospitality, health care, information technology, education and mass media, just to name a few. More than half of all new immigrants to Canada make their home in Ontario. The population of 12 million includes people from 200 countries who speak as many as 130 languages. *(Hmm...maybe a lot of them would like to read this book!)*

If you are a tourist visiting Ontario with children, you will definitely want to visit Canada's Premier Amusement Park – Canada's Wonderland. It has 16 roller coasters! The Leviathan is one of the tallest and fastest coasters in the world. Splash Works Water Park, live entertainment and a variety of special events provide lots of thrills for the whole family. So head for Vaughan, just north of the City of Toronto, and you may use its Internet site to make your plans. *(By the way - it's ok to visit without kids!)*

canadaswonderland.com

Did you know ...

* Professional sports are very "big" in Ontario. Football fans enjoy the Hamilton Tiger Cats, the Toronto Argonauts and the Ottawa Redblacks. The Toronto Blue Jays is its baseball team, and the Toronto Raptors its basketball team. The two hockey teams are the Toronto Maple Leafs and the Ottawa Senators. Ontario even has a professional Lacrosse team called Toronto Rock. *(I don't watch a lot of sports on TV, but my friends know not to interrupt me when I watch Saturday night's "Hockey Night in Canada!" Go Leafs, Go! Actually, when the 2010 Winter Olympics were in British Columbia, I watched a lot of sports then! Oh, and also when the Toronto Blue Jays were in the World Series in 2015. Did you see any of those games? They were spectacular!)*

* The SkyDome in Toronto opened in 1989 and was the first stadium in the world to have a fully retractable roof. It also has the largest JumboTron at 10 metres x 33.6 metres. If you're trying to find it in your tourist guidebook, it has been renamed the Rogers Centre. *(But all of us sports fans still call it the SkyDome.)*

* Ottawa is known as the "most educated city in Canada." More than 50% of the population has a college degree. Per capita, Ottawa has the highest number of scientists, PhDs, and engineers in the country. *(Sounds like education is a great pursuit in Ottawa.)*

The changing of the Guard, Parliament Hill, Ottawa

* With their tall copper roofs and Gothic structure, Canada's Parliament Buildings in Ottawa are an impressive sight and a symbol of national pride. *(Be sure to visit when you are in Ottawa!)*

* The "Group of Seven" and Tom Thomson were artists in the mid 1900s. They became famous for shifting the emphasis on imitating natural effects toward the expression of their feelings for their subjects. *(I like the details in the evergreen trees and all the shades of colour.)*

**Autumn Hillside (1920) by Franklin
Carmichael of the Group of Seven**

* The 5 Great Lakes make up the largest body of freshwater in the world. They are Superior, Huron, Erie, Ontario and Michigan. Even though Lake Michigan is wholly in the USA, it is still part of the same body of water as Lake Huron. *(Crossing the five-mile long Mackinac Bridge that joins Michigan's two peninsulas is quite an adventure because it really sways – a lot! - in the wind!)*

* William Neilson of Almonte, Ontario, wasn't a successful machinist so he decided to buy some cows and an old hand-turned ice cream maker. By 1915, he was selling a million pounds of ice cream and half a million pounds of candy a year. When his son took over the business, he introduced the Jersey Milk Chocolate Bar. He ran a contest that offered a Jersey cow as the prize. We don't know what the winner did with the cow but we know that Neilson's Jersey Milk bar became the company's all-time bestseller. *(Amazing what owning Jersey cows can lead to, isn't it?)*

* Toronto's CN Tower, one of the world's highest structures, is about one half a mile high. If you take The EdgeWalk, you will do a hands-free walk 116 stories above the ground. Attached to an overhead safety rail, you can push your personal limits and lean over Toronto with nothing but air and breathtaking views of Lake Ontario beneath you. Wow! *(Not sure I could do this! Well, I might try. Would you?)*

* The CN Tower also has the 360 Restaurant that provides great food to enjoy while having a revolving view of Toronto. The restaurant is just 350 metres above the ground. *(I think I could go that high especially inside the tower!)*

* With two-thirds of the province covered with forest and one sixth covered with water, Ontario is a happy home for mosquitoes. In Upsala, a small community near Thunder Bay, there is a giant mosquito statue. The mosquito is holding a knife and fork in one set of legs and a man with the other legs! Just google Upsala statue and you'll see it!

**Built in 1976, this communications and observation tower remains
the tallest free-standing structure in the Western Hemisphere**

* A visit to Upper Canada Village (founded in 1961) will let you step back in time to the 1860s. You can walk through over forty authentic buildings and hear the history of the area from costumed interpreters. Plan your tour through one of the largest living-history sites in Canada by using its website: uppercanadavillage.com

* The Upsala mosquito may be big, but I think the Canada goose on the Trans Canada Highway near Wawa, Ontario is even bigger! Apparently, this is the most photographed landmark in North America! The 8.5 metre

statue was first made of wire and plaster in 1960 to mark the completion of the Trans Canada Highway between Wawa and Sault Ste. Marie. However, the poor bird could not withstand the harsh winters of Northern Ontario and was replaced in 1963 with this metal statue. It is appropriate to "belong" to the town of Wawa whose name comes from the Ojibwe word for "wild goose." *(The scarf is to keep him warm in winter, eh?)*

Manitoba Provincial Flower

Prairie Crocus

Jane Crosby, 2016, watercolour, 22 x 11 cm

9

Manitoba (MB) – Canada's Keystone Province

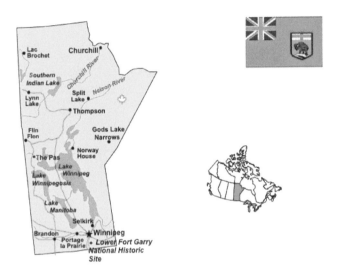

Population: 1,213,815 (2011)   Joined Confederation: July 15, 1870

Main Cities: Winnipeg (Capital), Brandon, Churchill, Dauphin, Selkirk, Steinbach, The Pas, Thompson

Places to Visit/Things to See:

Lower Fort Garry Historic Site   The Royal Winnipeg Ballet
The Forks Natural Historic Site
Royal Aviation Museum of Western Canada

Manitoba is the easternmost prairie province in Canada and is at the geographical centre of the country. It has an area of about 6000 square kilometres and is often called the "Land of 100,000 Lakes." It has a continental climate, which means it has great extremes of heat and cold. Summers are warm throughout the province but short in the north. It doesn't get a lot of rainfall, but enough to keep the soil good for growing crops. *(The "no-see-ums" - also known as midges - and mosquitos are very plentiful in wooded areas near all those lakes!)*

Falcon Lake, one of the 100,000 lakes in Manitoba

History

The name "Manitoba" probably comes from the Cree words "Manitou bau" which mean "Strait of the Spirit" or "Narrows of the Great Spirit." The name refers to the narrow part of Lake Manitoba. When the lake's waves break on the loose surface rocks of the north shore, they make an odd wailing sound. Early Aboriginal Peoples thought this was the sound of the Great Spirit Manitou beating on a huge drum.

Manitoba adjoins Hudson Bay to the northeast, and is the only prairie province to have a saltwater coastline. It is at the heart of the giant Hudson Bay watershed, once known as Rupert's Land. It was a vital area of the Hudson's Bay Company, with many rivers and lakes that provided excellent opportunities for the important fur trade.

The first inhabitants in the Manitoba region arrived about 10,000 years ago and were probably hunters following the buffalo. Early Inuit lived in the far north about 3,000 years ago. By the early 17th century, many Aboriginal groups occupied the Manitoba region. They included the Ojibwa, Cree, Dene, Sioux, Mandan and Assiniboine Peoples who founded settlements around the area. The first farming in Manitoba was along the Red River, where corn and other seed crops were planted before contact with Europeans.

In the late 1600s, explorers came looking for furs and a British fur-trading company called the Hudson's Bay Company (HBC), began to build forts. In 1670, King Charles II of Britain granted the HBC control over the area known as Rupert's Land. This covered an area of 3.9 million square km, over one-third the area of Canada today. *(That was definitely a large "gift" to one company from the British King!)*

In the 1730s, the French began exploring the Red River Valley and started building forts. In 1812 Selkirk settlers came to the Red River area. This was the same Lord Selkirk who had brought Scottish settlers to Prince Edward Island in 1803. *(You first found Lord Selkirk in Chapter 6.)*

The Red River Cart – the method used to travel for early settlers in Manitoba

The Red River Cart was a fantastic feat of engineering, as it used no metal! Many of these wagons carried the settlers' worldly goods on their journey westward. *(Can you imagine putting all your possessions in this cart?)*

Selkirk had a vision of a new colony at the centre of North America. He may not have seen that this would lead to the end of the fur trade's role in the country's economy. It was the beginning of the demographic and social transformation of western Canada. *(Today we can say "Many thanks, Lord Selkirk! But I imagine the fur traders were not very happy about those changing times.)*

In 1870, the British Crown paid the Hudson's Bay Company 1.5 million dollars [£300,000] to take back control of Rupert's Land. For 22 years the fur trade had dominated this land. Over the next 100 years, settlers from eastern Canada and Eastern Europe eventually created a sound agricultural tradition in Manitoba. *(I'm so glad Canada welcomed a lot of farmers to this new land!)*

Of all Canadian provinces, Manitoba contains the largest diversity of ethnic origins and the largest French community west of the Great Lakes. By 1875, when the beaver pelt was replaced by wheat, farming became a main contribution to the economy. Manufacturing and mining grew large in the 1900s, as did the production of hydroelectric power.

One cannot write about Manitoba without mentioning Louis Riel, the Métis spokesman. (The Métis are Indigenous North Americans of mixed race, generally from unions of Aboriginal women and European men.) Louis Riel was regarded as the founder of Manitoba, teacher, and leader of the North West Rebellion. The Métis people considered him a hero but many others named him a traitor. He was a visionary who wanted equal rights with English and French speaking people in Manitoba. In 1869, he wrote a List of Rights before Manitoba was to join confederation. A group of Loyalists in the territory saw this list, and the fact that Riel had set up a provisional government, as evidence of sedition. Riel was hanged as a traitor Nov. 16, 1885. Discussion continues to the present day. Was Riel a heroic freedom fighter who stood up for his people in the face of racist bigotry, or were his acts those of a traitor to his country? Read more and form your opinion online at: thecanadianencyclopedia.ca *(I believe this was a very sad event in our history.)*

The Great Depression (1929-1939) hit especially hard in Western Canada, including Manitoba. The world market collapsed and widespread drought devastated farmlands. When Canada entered World War II, Winnipeg became a major base for training fighter pilots and the 1940s provided jobs.

In the 1950s and 1960s Winnipeg and surrounding Red River Valley suffered major floods. It took six years to build the "Red River Floodway" - dikes and diversion dams to protect the Winnipeg area. In 1997, the "Flood of the Century" caused over $400 million in damages in Manitoba, but the floodway saved Winnipeg from flooding. *(Flooding occurs often in Southern Manitoba, especially in the spring when a lot of melting snow makes the rivers overflow.)*

Manitoba Today

Winnipeg is the capital of Manitoba and the geographical centre of North America. It lies at the spot where the Red and Assiniboine Rivers come together. This downtown area, known as The Forks, has been called the Cultural Capital of Canada. More than 100 languages are spoken in a variety of cultures. It is host to world-class ballet, theatre, visual arts, music and festivals while still being known as quite an affordable city. *(That's important because these days, most large cities in Canada are definitely not affordable.)*

This area in downtown Winnipeg has been a meeting place for thousands of years!

One of the amazing cultural events you may see at The Forks is native Hoop Dancing. It's absolutely breath taking! Just Google Canadian native hoop dancing for videos! *(I remember watching hoop dancing for the first time when visiting The Forks. I was in awe...probably because as a child I could barely master only one hoop! Do you remember the Hoola Hoop craze?)*

This amazing activity requires rhythm and tremendous concentration!

The northern port of Churchill is the only arctic deep-water port in Canada and the shortest shipping route between North America and Asia. Hudson Bay is the second-largest bay in the world. Tourists travel there in June/July to get up close to beluga whales in the Churchill River. Many tourists arrive in October/November to see polar bears.

Winnipeg announced exciting news of international significance in August 2015! Scientists in Canada's National Microbiology lab in Winnipeg had developed an experimental Ebola vaccine. In a trial in West Africa, all 2,014 vaccinated subjects showed no signs of the virus 10 days after vaccination. *(What a breakthrough of hope!)*

Did you know ...

* In 1914, WWI Captain Harry Colebourn took a black bear he named Winnie (after his hometown Winnipeg), to England as his Regiment's mascot. When he shipped out to France, he donated the bear to the London Zoo. Author A. A. Milne's son, Christopher, so loved the bear that Milne wrote stories about his boy and the bear, "Winnie the Pooh."

(Have you seen the movie recently released about Winnie's 'cousin' Paddington Bear? It is becoming a family favourite.)

* What do Bugs Bunny, Brad Pitt, James Bond and the song *American Woman* all have in common? Winnipeg, of course! Bugs was the creation of the Winnipeg cartoonist Charlie Thorson; Brad Pitt starred in *The Assassination of Jesse James by the Coward Robert Ford* filmed in Winnipeg, and *American Woman* was composed by Berton Cummings and made famous by the Winnipeg band *The Guess Who*.

* Winnipeg's contribution to popular music includes rockers Neil Young, Berton Cummings *(The Guess Who)*, Randy Bachman *(Bachman, Turner, Overdrive)*, the *Crash Test Dummies*, the *Watchmen*, Chantal Kreviazuk, Lenny Breau, the *Weakerthans*, *The Waking Eyes*, The *Wailin' Jennys*, *Bif Naked*, Ray St. Germain, Sierra Noble and many others. *(Guess that's enough for this paragraph! I hope you know some of them! If not, check them out on YouTube!)*

* The Second World War's most famous spymaster, Sir William Stephenson, the man called "Intrepid," was the inspiration for Ian Fleming's character 007 – James Bond. Stephenson was born and raised in Winnipeg. *(I still enjoy the James Bond movies, do you? I think the more modern movies that are similar are the Mission Impossible ones in which Tom Cruise stars. Have you seen any of them?)*

* In 1957, Winnipeg became the first North American city to adopt the 911 emergency phone numbers. They are now dialed around the world in an emergency situation. *(I didn't know that people in Canada have been dialing 911 for almost 60 years! I've only had to call it twice. How about you?')*

* Aboriginal Peoples Television Network, headquartered in Winnipeg, is the first national Aboriginal network in the world.

* Where to see a **Bolingbroke** or a **Westland Lysander**? These World War II training planes are in the Commonwealth Air Training Plan Museum in Brandon, MB. The museum, located at the Brandon Municipal Airport, is a registered historic site. See some great pictures online here:

airmuseum.ca *(This is for all you airplane fans!)*

* Winnipeg produces over 25,000 pounds of gold medal-winning Golden Caviar and sells it to some of the best restaurants worldwide. *(Actually the sturgeon, a freshwater fish, produces the roe (caviar) and Winnipeg puts it in tins!)*

* Winnipeg's Exchange District - the original centre of commerce and culture in Winnipeg - is designated as a National Historic Site. This is due to its rich collection of turn-of-the-last-century terracotta and stone cut buildings. They are unrivalled in all of North America. This is the area where the movies "Shall We Dance?" (starring Jennifer Lopez and Richard Gere) and "Capote" (starring Phillip Seymour Hoffman) were filmed. "

* The same architects who designed Grand Central Terminal in New York City, USA, designed Winnipeg's Union Station. *(I think many train stations across Canada look very similar to Winnipeg's.)*

Union Station, Winnipeg, Manitoba

Waterfront Station, Vancouver, British Columbia

Saskatchewan Provincial Flower

Western Red Lily
Jane Crosby, 2015, watercolour 25 x 18 cm

10

Saskatchewan (SK) – Land of Living Skies

Population: 1,114,170 (2013)   Joined Confederation: September 1, 1905

Main Cities: Regina (capital), Estevan, Moose Jaw, North Battleford, Prince Albert, Saskatoon, Swift Current, Yorkton

Towns: Aberdeen, Canora, Carrot, Flin Flon, Kindersley, Scott

Places to Visit/Things to See:

Grasslands National Park   RCMP Museum and Training Academy
Saskatchewan Air Show   Wanuskewin Heritage Park
Regina Globe Theatre   Cypress Hills Vineyard and Winery
MacKenzie Art Gallery   Ukrainian Museum of Canada

History

One of the three "Prairie Provinces," Saskatchewan is the easiest province to draw. It's just 4 straight lines that don't zig-zag along coastal waterways or go around mountains! It's the only province with entirely man-made boundaries. It was created, by carving land from the Northwest Territories.

Its name came from a Cree word meaning "swiftly flowing river." Evidence of Aboriginal inhabitants can be traced to at lease 10,000 BC when hunters followed the migratory herds of bison (buffalo). These various indigenous groups had created self-sustaining societies. As in other provinces, they are now referred to as "First Nations people."

The three main language groups of First Nations people each occupied about one third of the land. They had considerable influence on the names of various places in the province. The tribes living close to waterways were in contact with white men as early as 1690. Exploration continued in the 18th and 19th centuries and by 1870 the prairie land was crisscrossed by well-worn trails. *(Apparently some of those old routes are still visible from the air.)*

Fur traders were the first European explorers to arrive and small communities developed around the trading posts in the 1700s. The felt hat was very fashionable in Europe in the late 17th century and the best felt came from beaver. The first settlers had close ties to Britain, hence the names given to two major cities - Regina, and Prince Albert. They also named many of the 100,000 lakes and rivers in the province! *(The British chose names like Churchill Lake, and Milton Lake probably to remind them of home. Reindeer Lake, Round Lake and Mud Lake likely reflected the new land they were in. That's just my own theory!)*

After the railway was completed in the south of the province in 1883, many European settlers travelled west. Time, social mobility and intermarriage have blurred the lines separating the original settlements. Even into the 1980s, however, many parts of the province were still seen as being inhabited by specific groups – Doukhobors (a sect of Russian dissenters), German, French, Ukrainian, Scandinavian, Hutterite and Mennonite.

In Saskatchewan today, you can still hear the languages of Cree and Ojibwa spoken. Over 90% of Saskatchewanians are English speaking, about 1% is French speaking and over 6% speak other languages.

Over the decades, agriculture became the largest single industry in Saskatchewan. Wheat output steadily increased and the province is now one of the largest wheat producers in the world. Other grains, petroleum and potash also contributed to the economy.

A harvest of hay in Qu'appelle Valley, Saskatchewan

Saskatchewan Today

In years past, Saskatchewan had many unique grain elevators to store the prairie grain harvests. They were usually built next to the railway so they could empty the grain into rail cars. These days, the rural people have moved to urban areas and the grain elevators are disappearing. Check out their distinctive shapes and history online. *(Both the disappearing coastal lighthouses and prairie grain elevators are changing Canada's landscape.)*

The vanishing Grain Elevator – a symbol of days gone by

Most people live in the cities and towns in the southern part of the province. Many places have interesting names like Swift Current, Yorkton, North Battleford and Flin Flon.

> Saskatoon – the city, is also the name of a delicious berry
> Moose Jaw – came from a Cree word "Moosegaw" meaning
> "warm breezes"

Saskatchewan was the first province to promote multiculturalism. It desired its citizens to have an equal celebration of racial, religious and cultural backgrounds. All cultures come together during the province's two major multicultural festivals, the Folkfest in Saskatoon and the Mosaic in Regina.

These multi-day festivals feature pavilions, each devoted to a different nationality or culture. Visiting the pavilions is like going on a world tour. You can experience the music, dance, food, and history of many different cultural groups in just a few hours. For example, one specific festival in Saskatoon in May, the Vesna Festival, celebrates the Ukrainian culture.

Saskatchewan owes much of its orderly settlement in the 1880s to the North West Mounted Police. They were the "face" of Ottawa's desire for "peace, order and good government." Renamed the Royal Canadian Mounted Police in 1920, their red coats are recognized around the world. When you visit Regina be sure and stop into the RCMP training site. You can also check it out from home online here: rcmp-grc.gc.ca

When in Regina, you could also catch a football game with the Saskatchewan Roughriders and perhaps their biggest rival, the Winnipeg Blue Bombers. If you are in southern Saskatchewan and want to pop over the border into the USA, you could visit the States of North Dakota and/ or Montana.

From symphony orchestras to country music, from art galleries and live theatre, Saskatchewan invites visitors to experience a variety of the visual arts. Two small Saskatchewan towns are home to the long-running Canadian television sitcoms *Corner Gas* and *Little Mosque on the Prairie.* They poked fun at prairie life and gaining mutual understanding of two cultures. *(When in Canada you can catch reruns on CTV and The Comedy Network.)*

The novels of W.O. Mitchell *(Who Has Seen the Wind)* and Guy Vanderhaeghe *(The Englishman's Boy)* are set in Saskatchewan. Farley Mowat lived in Saskatoon at times and wrote wonderful children's novels of the sea and the plains. Children's titles include *The Boat Who Wouldn't Float, The Dog Who Wouldn't Be* and *Owls in the Family.*

Buffy Sainte-Marie is a Canadian Cree singer-songwriter, musician, educator and social activist. In all of these areas her work has focused on issues of Indigenous people of the Americas. She has won many awards and honours for both her music and her work in education and social activism. She was born in Qu'Appelle Valley, Saskatchewan.

The Saskatchewan Legislative Building and grounds were designated a National Historic Site of Canada in 2005. Of historical significance, the table that was used during the meeting of the Fathers of Confederation in Québec City in 1864 is in the building's library.

Saskatchewan's Legislative Building in Regina

Tourism Saskatchewan promises "urban excitement, rural relaxation, wilderness exploration, and parkland peace and quiet." Wherever your sense of adventure takes you, you'll find a warm Saskatchewan welcome.

Did you know ...

* In 2010, from a list of 10 nominees in a cross-Canada survey, former Premier of Saskatchewan, Tommy Douglas, was voted "The Greatest Canadian." He was Premier from 1944 to 1961 and is considered the Father of Medicare, Canada's Health Care System. Read more about this fascinating man online here: thecanadianencyclopedia.ca

* E. Pauline Johnson was a popular writer and performer in the late 19th century. Her father was a hereditary Mohawk chief of mixed ancestry and her mother was an English immigrant. Johnson was noted for her poems and performances that celebrated her Aboriginal heritage. Just google her name on the Internet to find more. *(I like these lines from one of her best known poems, The Song My Paddle Sings.)*

> *And up on the hills against the sky,*
> *A fir tree rocking its lullaby,*
> *Swings, swings,*
> *Swelling the song that my paddle sings.*

* Sharon Butala is one of Canada's finest short story writers *(Real Life)*. Max Braithwaite was a novelist and non-fiction author known for his humour *(Never Sleep Three in a Bed)*. Yann Martel wrote the prize-winning bestseller *Life of Pi*. These authors all live in Saskatchewan.

* The Snowbirds, the Canadian Air Force's premier military aerobatics display team, have their home 5 minutes south of Moose Jaw. Citizens of Moose Jaw are often treated to a mini air show when the Snowbirds practice their maneuvers over the city.

* You could spend the day seeing the sights of Moose Jaw in a trolley car. Instead, you could spend time at a u-pick orchard getting your fill of cherries, raspberries, plums, haskaps and Saskatoon berries. *(I had no idea what those last two berries were so I "googled" them. I found that haskaps are the berries of the edible blue honeysuckle plant. Haskap is a Japanese name meaning"berry of long life and good vision." The Saskatoon berry'is similar to the blueberry but has a unique subtle flavour of a "wild" fruit. If you only have blueberries you could still make good muffins!)*

Haskap berries

Saskatoon berries

* You could have fun "Geocaching" in Saskatchewan! Saskatoon has over 400 caches hidden thoroughout the city providing wonderful challenges and great scenery along the riverbank. *(Oops – you don't know about Geocaching? Neither did I! I found it on the Internet here: geocaching.com)*

* Sports are very big in Saskatchewan. Although they have no professional hockey team, the province boasts having a North American Hockey legend, the big Detroit Red Wings #9 - Gordie Howe. He was born in Floral, Saskatchewan and became known fondly as "Mr. Hockey." There is a bridge being planned to connect Windsor, Ontario, Canada and Detroit, Michigan, USA, by the year 2020. It will be known as the Gordie Howe International Bridge. *(That's quite a legacy to honour a wonderful gentleman from a small Saskatchewan town.)*

* A Saskatchewan women's curling team has won **three** world titles and in 1998 went on to win the **first** Olympic Gold medal ever to be awarded for curling. *(This sport has some fascinating history and many of our best Canadian players come from Saskatchewan. Do you curl?)*

* Catriona Le May Doan, was born in Saskatoon in 1970. She is a speed skater, and a double Olympic champion in the 500 m, and has been named the "fastest woman on ice." You can see the many records she has broken and medals she has won if you go on the Internet here: Catriona_LeMay_ Doan *(Check YouTube too!)*

* Hockey player, Hayley Wickenheiser, is the pride of Shaunavon, Saskatchewan. She received her fourth career gold medal when the Team Canada Women's Hockey Team won over the Americans in a heart-stopping 3-2 overtime Olympic final in Feb. 2014. Hayley was the first woman to play full-time professional ice hockey in a position other than goalie. She has won four Olympic medals – three gold and one silver. *(It was so exciting to watch that Olympic final game in 2014! Did you see it?)*

* Joni Mitchell is a singer/songwriter whose music continues to resonate with fans both old and new. Have you ever heard her songs "Put Up a Parking Lot" or "Big Yellow Taxi"? Perhaps you might prefer the country music sound of Alex Runions from Regina?

* Michif is the unique language of the Métis, created through the blending of French and Cree words. Teaching Aboriginal languages in First Nations and provincial schools is becoming more common now. *(Thankfully, First Nations languages and cultures are being preserved.)*

* The hottest temperature ever recorded in Canada was in Saskatchewan. The temperature rose to 45 °C in Midale and Yellow Grass. The coldest temperature ever recorded in the province was −56.7 °C in Prince Albert, which is north of Saskatoon.

Alberta Provincial Flower

Wild Rose

Jane Crosby, 2015, watercolour 20 x 24 cm

11

Alberta (AB) – Wild Rose Country

Population: 4,082,571   Joined Confederation: September 1, 1905

Cities: Calgary, Edmonton (Capital), Leduc, Lethbridge, Medicine Hat, St. Albert

Towns: Banff, Canmore, Cochrane Drumheller, Okotoks, Olds, Pincher Creek

Places to Visit/Things to See:

Banff & Jasper National Parks   The Calgary Stampede
The world's largest Easter Egg   Tubing in Canmore
Dinosaur Provincial Park   Canadian Badlands Passion Play

History

Alberta is one of only 2 provinces in Canada that are landlocked. Look at the map of Canada and see if you can find the other one? *(Hint: Go east from Alberta.)* With almost four million residents, Alberta has the largest population of the three Prairie Provinces. *(Manitoba, Saskatchewan and Alberta are known as Canada's three Prairie Provinces.)*

The original inhabitants of the Alberta land were First Nations people. They had traversed the land 11,000 years before the first white men arrived. It is thought many tribes had migrated to this region from Eastern Saskatchewan and Ontario because they spoke languages similar to Algonquian. These ancestors to the Algonquian people were referred to as the Blackfoot Nation. They were hunting for large game such as buffalo. Written history of the province only began with the Europeans' arrival.

In the late 1700s, the Blackfoot people were using horses that they captured in raids or trades with the natives from the American lands to the south. There were no real boundaries between north and south in the area of Alberta. Many native tribes hunted on the northern Plains of present day Alberta and as far south as present day Wyoming, USA.

The fur trade brought the English and French westward. After the French were defeated at the fall of Québec in 1759, the **H**udson's **B**ay **C**ompany (HBC) really pushed its monopoly on the fur trade. *(Remember, they got that huge area of Rupert's Land as a 'gift' from King Charles II of Britain in 1670?)* By the 1770s, the HBC was being challenged by the **N**orth **W**est **C**ompany (NWC), a private Montréal-based company that hoped to recreate the old French trading network. *(Tension was growing between these two companies!)*

An Alberta "soddy" – a new settler's first home

Many of Alberta's cities and towns, including Fort Edmonton, started as either Hudson's Bay Company or North West Company trading posts. The two companies merged in 1821, and in 1870 the new HBC's trade monopoly was abolished and the region was wide open to entrepreneurs. Enter the brand new Dominion of Canada (1867)! In 1868 all of Rupert's Land and the North-Western Territory were given to Canada and became *(you guessed it!)* the Northwest Territories!

You *can* experience life and the fur trade in the 1800s! Visit the Fort George and Buckingham House Provincial Historic Site. It's a short trip east from Edmonton to Elk Point. You could also get more information here: history.alberta.ca/fortgeorge

In the 1870s, the **N**orth-**W**est **M**ounted **P**olice (NWMP) force was established and just in time to deal with those pesky US whiskey traders causing trouble in Fort Whoop-Up. *(No kidding, that was a real name!)* The force became world famous not only for keeping order during the Klondike Gold Rush, but also for being a part of the Canadian Siberian Expeditionary Force sent to Russia in 1918.

The force was busy keeping peace and order along the Canadian Pacific Railway line. The line kept moving west finally reaching Calgary in 1883. The North West Mounted Police became the **Royal Canadian Mounted Police** in 1920. They are affectionately called "The Mounties" by – well – the world! They have appeared in many "historical" movies made by American film companies. *(I think maybe it's these movies rather than knowledge of our history that has made the Canadian Mountie known around the world!)* See more here:

rcmp-grc.gc.ca/en/why-be-part-musical-ride

Today's Royal Canadian Mounted Police

There was a huge fire in 1886 that destroyed 14 buildings in downtown Calgary and no one was injured. However, city officials drafted a law requiring all large downtown buildings to be built with Paskapoo sandstone to prevent this from happening again. *(If you are interested in archeology, you might want to check out Paskapoo's fossil record.)*

Alberta Today

Calgary is Alberta's largest city, but Edmonton is the capital. It is the service hub for Canada's crude oil and oil sands (see Athabasca Oil Sands). The northern resource industries rely on Edmonton for supplies. Alberta has a worldwide reputation in the area of cold weather construction and green building technologies. They stress a priority on quality, energy conservation and making efficient use of sustainable resources.

The XV Olympic Winter Games were held in Calgary in 1988. Some people remember them for the debut of the Jamaica national bobsled team! The five purpose-built venues are being used to train Canadian athletes, among them, those who won 26 medals in the 2010 Winter Olympics in Vancouver, British Columbia. *(I volunteered in the Athletes Village during those Olympics and saw many world class Olympians up close! The whole city seemed like one big family! The greatest thrill was watching our Canadian athletes win gold! Did you see any of those Olympic events in Vancouver or on TV?)*

Alberta offers many tourist attractions. If water sports are your interest, you might like to take a white water rafting adventure in Jasper National Park, Alberta. *(Sure looks like fun!)*

Photo courtesy of Jasper's Whitewater Rafting Company

If skiing is your sport, you will want to visit Lake Louise in Banff National Park. It's one of Canada's most awesome picture-taking sites and the ski hills are world famous. Hiking through Banff National Park is great in winter or summer but be on the lookout for mountain goats and bears! See some pictures here: skilouise.com

Alberta has over 9000 farms that produce grain crops such as wheat and canola. It also has a reputation for raising excellent livestock (steers, calves, pigs, poultry, etc.) The province exports over 75% of its beef to the USA.

Alberta is the province that hosts the annual Calgary Stampede, the highest grossing festival in Canada. It's a huge annual festival of events that attracts visitors from around the world every July. Over one million people attend the 10-day event that features one of the world's largest rodeos. It's interesting to note that barrel racing is the only event in the Stampede that is open to women. *(I have attended a few small rodeos over the years, and the Stampede is on my future "must see" list. Isn't the sense of motion in this steer-roping picture awesome?)* Check it out here: calgarystampede.com

Steer roping at the Calgary Stampede
- Christopher Martin Photography, Used with permission.

Barrel racing at the Calgary Stampede

Did you know ...

* Alberta has some strange names for cities – like Red Deer, Medicine Hat and Wood Buffalo! *(They should have a names competition with Newfoundland!)*

* It would be fun to explore Head Smashed in Buffalo Jump – it's a UNESCO World Heritage Site in southern Alberta. You can learn more here:

  history.alberta.ca/headsmashedin

* Allie Bertram, born in Calgary, is a trained classical dancer and actress who is now a mermaid! Well, not a real one, but she plays Mimmi, the newest mermaid in the popular Australian television series *Mako Mermaids. (You can watch the series on Netflix!)*

* Another UNESCO World Heritage Site is the Dinosaur Provincial Park. Located about a half hour drive southeast of Calgary, it is one of the richest dinosaur fossil locales in the world. If you are excited to see *chasmosaurus bellis*, then be sure to visit this Park! Make sure you also check out the hoodoos in the badlands! You can see more here:

  albertaparks.ca/dinosaur.aspx

* Scientists predict that 20 percent of the arctic glaciers' ice mass will disappear by 2100. In Jasper and Banff National Parks, you can still see glaciers but they are slowly melting so you should come and see them while you can! *(They are really breathtaking!)*

* Alberta has the largest Easter Egg in the world – almost 8 m high! To celebrate the 100th anniversary of the North West Mounted Police in 1974, Vegreville erected the giant Ukrainian Easter Egg called a Pysanka (pronounced "PIH-sahn-kah). Alberta is home to many Ukrainians. Here's a picture of the huge egg!

The world's largest Pysanka

* Canada has three Prairie Provinces: Manitoba, Saskatchewan, and Alberta. Of the three, Alberta is the only one to border just a single U.S. state. Alberta borders on the state of Montana.

* Edmonton is the home of a National Hockey Team, the Edmonton Oilers. In the 1980s this team included Wayne Gretzky, or as hockey fans called him "the Great One"! *(#99!)* When Gretzky was with them, the team won the coveted Stanley Cup **four** times! On August 9, 1988, he was traded to the Los Angles Kings hockey team, and moved to the USA. *(And all Canada mourned its loss.)* However! In October 2016 Gretzky again became part of the Edmonton Oilers organization – although not on the ice. He will be the ambassador for the National Hockey League's 2017 centennial celebrations. *(Welcome back to Canada, #99!)*

* Kurt Browning, born in Rocky Mountain House, Alberta, was the first figure skater to land a quadruple jump in competition. *(That's 4 revolutions in the air. Phenomenal!)* That was 1988 and for the **next three years** he won Gold Medals in the World Figure Skating Championships. He is a member of the Canadian Sports Hall of Fame. *(And rightfully so!)*

* Alberta produces some great current country music artists like Brett Kissel from Flat Lake. Just to balance musical styles, the province has several opera companies and many symphony orchestras.

British Columbia Provincial Flower

Pacific Dogwood
Jane Crosby, 2015, watercolour 17 x 20 cm

British Columbia (BC) – Beautiful BC

Population: 4,700,000   Joined Confederation: July 20, 1871

Mainland Cities: Abbotsford, Burnaby, Kamloops, Kelowna, Prince George, Richmond, Surrey, Vancouver

Van. Island Cities: Victoria (Capital), Campbell River, Duncan, Esquimalt, Nanaimo, Port Alberni, Qualicum,

Places to Visit/Things to See: Vancouver Mainland

Mainland Museum of Anthropology   Granville Island   Steveston
Stanley Park Totems   Abbostsford Air Show
Okanagan Wine Tour   Whistler/Blackcomb Ski Site
Grouse Mountain & Capilano Canyon - North Van.

Places to Visit/Things to See: Vancouver Island

Butchart Gardens   Royal BC Museum   Empress Hotel
Nanaimo Bathtub Races   Cathedral Grove   Uculet (surfing)

While the capital, Victoria, is on Vancouver Island, British Columbia's largest city, Vancouver, is on the mainland of the province. I realize this Victoria/Vancouver/Island/Mainland bit can be confusing but I think looking at the map will help. *(I certainly hope so anyway!)*

British Columbia is Canada's west coast province. Queen Victoria named it in 1858 and the capital city is named after her. British Columbia is why we can say Canada extends "from sea to sea" – because Newfoundland is on the Atlantic Ocean and British Columbia is on the Pacific Ocean. There are about 4,440 km in between these provinces – a long drive or an eight-hour flight. *(I always thought Australia was huge but it only took a three and one half hour flight to cross the whole continent– from Perth to Sydney. What a surprise!)*

History

There is evidence people were living in British Columbia over 10,500 years ago. Over the centuries, the land and the climate affected the Aboriginal groups in different ways. Along the seacoast where the climate was mild and wet, enormous cedar, hemlock and spruce trees grew in large numbers. They provided planks for houses, bark and roots to weave clothing, fishnets, mats and baskets. The cedar trees were made into large canoes and totem poles that were so important to First Nations' culture.

An elaborately painted Haida Canoe

Totem Poles in Stanley Park

Like other coastal people, the Nuu-cha-nulth (means "all along the mountains") made their living from the sea. However, this group on the west coast of Vancouver Island became known for their special skill - hunting the huge grey whale - with harpoons. The meat and oil were food and the bone made tools and utensils. There was always a big celebration as the whale was shared with the whole village. *(Always lots to eat for all!)*

In the interior of the province where the climate was drier, it was much colder in the winter and hotter in the summer. The people lived in small family groups and moved around to gather berries and roots and to hunt deer, moose and caribou. Salmon was an important food fished from the freshwater streams. *(Salmon is still an important food source enjoyed throughout BC.)*

In 1778 the Nu-cha-nulth people met Captain James Cook when he explored the coast for the King of England. Trade with the Aboriginal groups flourished but confusion began over who actually "owned" the land. The Spanish wanted to expand from Mexico to the north. The Russians were planning expeditions from their posts in Alaska, and the British claimed the land for Great Britain because of Captain Cook's visits. Then, to enforce Britain's claim to ownership, along came Captain George Vancouver in 1792 with orders to survey the coastline of North America between California and Alaska. *(Who 'owned' what land and what traders could travel through created a lot of tension.)*

Vancouver and his crew spent three summers on the rugged coast and drew the first accurate map of the British Columbia shoreline. Eventually the Russians and Spanish withdrew and although the land 'belonged' to Great Britain anyone could trade on the coast. Of course, no one asked the Aboriginal people. They knew the land belonged to them. After all, their ancestors had lived there for thousands of years. This different view of land ownership continues to the present and has resulted in Aboriginal land claim issues not only in British Columbia but all across Canada. *(See the Nunavut chapter.)*

In 1793, Aboriginal guides helped Alexander Mackenzie cross the formidable Rocky Mountains and become the first person to cross North America from the east to the Pacific Ocean. Simon Fraser followed in 1805, and the famous United States' Lewis and Clark expedition reached present day Portland, Oregon in 1806. In 1858, a stampede of 30,000 newcomers came to British Columbia looking for gold. A road 600 km long was built from Vancouver into the Interior. The mining town of Barkerville sprang up at the end of it. *(This "ghost town" is fun for tourists to visit today.)*

People in the Prairies began the horrendous journey to British Columbia to "strike it rich." They traveled by horseback, cart and foot over dusty sunbaked trails. One group of 150 people from Manitoba took 135 days to reach Kamloops, British Columbia. *(And they still had about 475 km to go to reach Barkerville!)* None of these "Overlanders" struck it rich, but many settled in British Columbia. *(I think the one-way trip was enough for them!)*

The gold rush changed British Columbia forever. The province provided much wealth to Britain from its gold, furs, timber for ships and masts, and coal to power the new coal-fired steam engines in British ships. But the colonists became increasingly unhappy. Should they become Americans? Should they become Canadians because there was talk of a railway going to link east and west? Should they stay a colony of Great Britain? I expect you've already guessed the answer! In July 1871, British Columbia became the 6th province of Canada. *(Yippee!)*

Work on the promised railway began in Yale, British Columbia in May 1879 and ended on Nov. 7, 1885. On the prairies, **10 km** of track could be laid every day. In BC it took 18 months to blast 4 tunnels to go just **2.5 km**. 17,000 Chinese labourers worked on the railway for $1/day. The railway was an iron thread attaching the Pacific province to the rest of Canada. All along the route, towns sprang into life. *(Nothing like a railway to 'open up' a country – or a province! British Columbians had to wait* 14 years *to see the promised railway! It must have been exciting to be the first train passengers!)*

A second railway was built through the north of British Columbia and helped create communities in the Interior. The man who envisioned making Prince Rupert an international seaport, Charles Hays, died in the sinking of the Titanic in April 1912. His dream for Prince Rupert died with him.

**Driving the Last Spike on the Canadian
Pacific Railway at Craigellachie, BC**

Canneries for salmon were busy along the coast and Aboriginal people came from all over the coast to work at them. Trees grew as tall as 30 story buildings and it took early hand-loggers many hours of hard work to chop one down. The explorer, David Thompson, wrote:

We are pygmies among the giant pines and cedars of this country.

Vancouver began as a small group of shacks huddled around a sawmill where ships from around the world came to load lumber. When gold ran out, coal became the "black gold" as British Columbians continued to rely for their livelihood on the natural resources of land and sea. Fish, timber and minerals became the foundation of the province's wealth. People in British Columbia became known as "hewers of wood and drawers of water." *(It took many years to overcome that assumption! I'm not sure it has entirely gone away.)*

A huge British Columbia Douglas fir tree

British Columbia Today

The canneries are gone from the coast but British Columbia still has a resource-based economy – principally logging, farming, and mining. Although they are diminishing, there are still forests of 100 year-old Douglas fir and cedar trees being logged. *(I have seen ONE Douglas fir tree that was so big it barely fit on ONE huge logging truck to bring it down the mountain! Our 5-year old son was very familiar with the huge BC trees. Passing a lumberyard during a visit to Ontario one summer, he saw a pile of "very skinny logs" and didn't know what they were! We assured him they were really trees but he called them "big toothpicks!")*

Immigration from mainly India and China has created an ever-growing multicultural population in British Columbia. More than 50,000 people come to Vancouver each year adding to the two and one half million people presently in greater Vancouver. By the end of the 1990s about 20% or one in five immigrants to British Columbia had come from Hong Kong, China, India, Japan and other Asian countries.

Since the International Exposition in 1986 and the Winter Olympics in 2010, tourism has boomed in the province. Tourists come to see some of the most spectacular mountain scenery in the world. Whistler, a two-hour drive north from Vancouver, is ranked as the #1 ski resort destination in North America. Many tourists stop over in Vancouver to enjoy world-class restaurants and shopping before boarding a cruise ship to take them up the coast to Alaska. *(I loved that spectacular cruise and learned much about Aboriginal cultures and the colossal glaciers.)* Many international students come to study in British Columbia's universities and colleges. Art and Culinary Institutes, Film Industry Programs, Health Sciences and Recreation Programs are offered on campuses and/or via the Internet.

Did you know ...

* The first automobile was seen in Vancouver about 1904. It rumbled through the streets at 10 km/hour, coughing smoke and frightening horses.

* One exotic product that came via ships from the orient was silk. Trains carried it to eastern Canada and the USA. Raw silk spoils very quickly so speed was crucial. When a train carrying silk was passing, all other traffic on the railway stopped. *(Yes, there were lots of "sidings" constructed. I wondered about there being more than one railroad track!)*

* The Lions Gate Bridge was built during the 1930s, partly to give jobs to unemployed people during the Depression. It's an historic landmark and connects downtown Vancouver via Stanley Park to the North Shore communities.

* A Canadian athlete, 19 year-old Terry Fox, dipped his artificial leg in the Atlantic Ocean in Newfoundland, April 12, 1980. He intended to run across Canada to raise money for cancer research. Sadly, his cancer returned and his selfless journey was halted September 1st near Wawa, Ontario. He had walked 5,373 km and he died June 28, 1981. Terry's "Marathon of Hope" has continued every September involving millions of participants in over 60 countries. It is now the world's largest one-day fundraiser for cancer research. To date over $700 million has been raised. *(For 5 months in 1980 the Canadian nation held its breath and focused on Terry's dream.)*

Terry on the road

"Somewhere the hurting must stop"

* Inspired by Terry Fox's courage, the "Man in Motion," Rick Hansen, travelled 40,073 km in his wheelchair through 34 countries. His dream was to help create "a world without barriers for people with disabilities." In his two-year tour, he wore out 117 wheelchair tires and 11 pairs of gloves. He raised $26 million for his cause and today the Rick Hansen Foundation raises millions more. It brings together experts to "accelerate progress in prevention, care and cure of paralysis after spinal cord injury."

(Terry and Rick are British Columbia's heroes.)

* Often called "Hollywood North," British Columbia has given us many popular culture actors and singers. If the names are not familiar to you, "Google" them and I'm sure you'll know a few! Michael J. Fox *(Back to the Future)*; Margo Kidder *(Superman); Chief Dan George (Little Big Man);* Jason Priestly *(Beverley Hills 90210),* and Hayden Christensen *(Star Wars).* Then check out musicians Joni Mitchell, Sarah McLachlan, Randy Bachman *(Bachman- Turner Overdrive)* and Michael Bublé. The pop-rock group Hedley and country artists Dean Brody and Dallas Smith are popular "BC boys."

* Thomas Dufferin ("Duff") Pattullo, British Columbia Premier 1933 – 1941, felt government should help the poorest members of society. He put unemployed people to work building roads and bridges and began a system of medical insurance. *(Google his name and you'll see 'his' bridge. I just had to put this in because he was my husband's relative ☺!)*

* The World Championship Bathtub race is held every year in Nanaimo, British Columbia. People flock from around the world to Vancouver Island to see this exciting event. Held the third week of July, it amazes everyone to see that bathtubs can really float. Add a motor and you have a bathtub race!

* In 1942, engineers and thousands of American soldiers built the 2,248 km Alaska-Canadian Highway from Dawson Creek, British Columbia, to Delta Junction, Alaska. During World War, II this was a route used to transport military supplies to U.S. bases in Alaska. *(Our son led bicycle groups on this highway every summer in 1993-2003. He said encountering black bears wasn't scary, but the gravel spun up by big RVs whizzing by on the gravel road was really frightening! It's all paved now.)*

* Much-loved British Columbia artist, Emily Carr, studied painting in London and Paris but found her inspiration in the tall forests and Aboriginal villages of the Pacific Coast. Her childhood home in Victoria is now a museum open to the public. You might like to visit the Art and Design School on Granville Island that is named after her. Carr wrote these inspirational words:

I glory in our wonderful west and I hope to leave behind me some of the relics of its first primitive greatness. These things should be to us Canadians what the ancient Briton's relics are to the English. Only a few more years and they will be gone forever into silent nothingness and I would gather my collection together before they are forever past.

Totems in an Aboriginal village in British Columbia - Emily Carr

Fireweed

Jane Crosby, 2015, watercolour 30 x 18 cm

13

Yukon (YT) – Canada's Smallest Northern Territory

Population: 33, 897   **Joined Confederation**: June 13, 1898

Main City: Whitehorse (capital)

Main Towns: Dawson, Faro, Haines Junction, Watson Lake

Places to Visit/Things to See:

White Water Rafting   Expeditions on the Tatshenshini River
Yukon Wildlife Preserve   Takhini Hot Pools

History

The history of humans living in the Yukon area dates back to the Ice Age. The original inhabitants are believed to have arrived over 20,000 years ago by migrating over the land bridge from Asia. The name Yukon comes from the Gwich'in word Yu-kun-ah meaning "great river," referring to the Yukon River.

The majority of Aboriginal peoples of Yukon belong to the Na-dene linguistic group that included about 10 different groups of hunter-gatherers.

The groups tended to blend into each other and they relied on salmon and caribou for food. In the far north, the Inuit have a different language and culture from the rest of Yukon's Aboriginal peoples. Because they live on the treeless Arctic slope, they have traditionally relied for food on fish and sea mammals.

It's interesting that the Yukon is one of the youngest parts of Canada to have seen European settlements. It is, however, the part of North America that has been continuously inhabited.

The first visitors to the northwest were Russian explorers who traveled along the Alaskan coast in the 18th century. Captain Bering, a Dane in the Russian navy, explored the Alaskan coast in 1741. He named Mt. Elias and told of large numbers of sea otters and other furbearing animals. This led to the spread of the Russian fur trade into the Alaska area. Alexander Mackenzie, one of Canada's greatest explorers, arrived on the Arctic coast in 1789.

Mt. St. Elias – the second highest mountain in Canada and the USA

In 1825, Sir John Franklin was searching for the Northwest Passage (a quick route to China) and mapped a lot of the Arctic coastline. In the 1840s, fur traders with the **H**udson's **B**ay **C**ompany (HBC) made the first lasting contact between Europeans and the Aboriginal people. Whalers had come to the north coast, missionaries followed them and then the **N**orth **W**est **M**ounted **P**olice came to Fort Selkirk and Herschel Island. Soon the Hudson's Bay Company set up posts along Yukon Rivers. The newcomers were not very welcome and one Aboriginal group ransacked

Fort Selkirk in 1852 and drove the Hudson's Bay Company out of southern Yukon.

In March 1867, Russia sold Alaska to the United States and many American traders moved into the Yukon area that was considered to be American territory. Hundreds of whalers spent the winters at Herschel Island and traded with Alaskan and Canadian Inuit for meat and furs. As they did elsewhere, the newcomers brought alcohol and devastating diseases to the Inuit people. *(A very sad legacy.)*

Anglican and Roman Catholic missionaries moved into the area in the 1860s. The Anglicans built schools in many areas. One story tells of Bishop William C. Bompass who served for many years. He became known as the "Bishop who ate his boots" as during one difficult and cold winter spell, when game was scarce, he did just that. *(I expect he had to boil them first!)*

"There's gold in the Yukon!" was the shout that sent thousands of adventurers to this small territory in 1896 to be part of the historic "Klondike Gold Rush." This era resulted in the creation of settlements, roads, businesses, and many colourful stories about the people and events in the region. *(Check out the poem "The Cremation of Sam McGee" by Canadian poet Robert W. Service. He is noted for his fictional poems and stories about the north.)*

Imagine that you are living in a small campsite and enjoying the peace and quiet, when suddenly, 30,000 people join you. Good-bye quiet campsite and hello noisy Dawson City! Instead of fishing you could hang out with your friends in dance halls and saloons! *(Wow! What a change that was!!)* Dawson grew to become the largest Canadian city west of Winnipeg.

Gold mining shifted to silver and lead production but a volatile world market for minerals made development and stability of the mining industry difficult. Then, in 1914, several hundred men from the Yukon population of 7,000 joined other Canadians to fight in the First World War. This had a terrible effect on the economy of the Yukon. Fur prices were climbing during the war years, however, and the fur trade became an important seasonal activity for the Aboriginal peoples – as well as for the prospectors. The fur trade attracted wealthy big-game hunters, which also helped the tourist industry.

Completed in 1900, the White Pass and Yukon railway connected Whitehorse, Yukon to Skagway on the Alaskan coast. Sternwheelers went up and down the Yukon and Stewart Rivers, carrying people and supplies between Whitehorse, Mayo and Dawson. *(The cross Canada railway had already been operating for 15 years.)*

Yukon has many plateaus and valleys, rivers and snow-capped mountains. Mount Logan (5,959 m) is the highest mountain in Canada and the second highest mountain in North America (after Mt. McKinley in Alaska, USA.) Mount St. Elias borders both the Yukon and Alaska and is the fourth highest in North America. This mountain region shares 600 km of interconnected lakes. *(They are glacial, which means you don't want to put even a toe in one of those lakes.)*

The beautiful Kluane Lake, Yukon

Most of the land in Yukon lies below the tree line, except the Arctic Coast. Because the summer seasons are short, the trees grow slowly and develop into hardy, high-quality wood. White spruce and lodgepole pine trees are of commercial interest. There are over 200 species of wildflowers in this

Territory. *(Few plant species are introduced and few could thrive in this extreme climate, yet invasive plants are a concern in the region.)*

Big game animals, furbearers, birds and fish have fed and clothed Yukon's Aboriginal peoples for thousands of years. They continue to be used today. The Yukon has large populations of Dall sheep that have thick, curled horns. There is also a large population of grizzly bears, one of the sheep's natural predators. The caribou and moose populations are so large there are more caribou and twice as many moose as people! *(The people don't seem to mind so I guess the moose don't either!)*

The permanent population of the Yukon continued to rise during the 1950s and 1960s and most of the economic activity was around Whitehorse. In 1953, the capital was moved south from Dawson City to Whitehorse.

The Yukon Today

Mount Logan, Yukon - Canada's highest mountain

The population of the Yukon in 2011 was 33,897. The population of Dawson City in the 2011 census was 1,319. Some 60,000 visitors each year come to see Yukon's fascinating historical sites, beautiful natural areas, and exciting cultural activities. The territory consists of towering mountain ranges, rolling plateaus, wide expanses of tundra, and rugged coastal areas. Outdoor enthusiasts from all over the world come to enjoy snowmobiling, backpacking and canoeing. *(The north has a beauty all its own. Have you ever travelled this far north?)*

The Yukon was originally part of the Northwest Territories but it became a separate territory in June 1898. Whitehorse, the capital, is known as the "Wilderness City" and is surrounded by hiking trails. The Yukon River flows right through the heart of the city. *(Very handy if you wanted a quick paddle in the early morning!)*

Today the mineral industry is the base of the Yukon's economy. Tourism, retail trade, government services, construction and fur production also support the economy.

Most of the Yukon is covered by permafrost, ground that remains frozen throughout the year. It lies just beneath a thin upper layer of ground called the active layer, which usually thaws in summer. Because the permafrost layer cannot absorb the water many swamps and bogs are formed. *(Good idea to keep your "Wellies" handy. That's British for rubber* boots. *)*

There is a specific hotel in Dawson City that has become famous for serving a drink called the Sourtoe Cocktail, which features a real mummified human toe. Yuk! The unique cocktail was introduced in 1973 and over 65,000 paying customers are reported to have tried the concoction. *(I think I'll pass... how about you?)*

Every February, Dawson City acts as the halfway mark for the Yukon Quest International Sled Dog Race. Mushers entered in the event, have a mandatory 36-hour layover in Dawson City. This allows them to get some rest and prepare for the second half of the world's toughest sled dog race. *(Note the 'boots' on the dog's paws. These keep their pads from freezing and cracking during the many miles they race over the sharp pieces of frozen snow and ice.)*
Check out great pictures here: yukonquest.com

A team leaves the Slaven's Cabin checkpoint of the Yukon Quest

The Yukon Transportation Museum in Whitehorse shows moose-skin boats, snowshoes, stagecoaches, dogsleds, and other early forms of transportation. *(I'd love to try a short trip by dogsled, wouldn't you?)*

The Yukon may be home to twice as many moose as people, but the 35,000 enterprising and creative folks who live here are exceptionally talented. Yukoners celebrate a varied history and a dynamic arts culture. The vast northern landscapes figure prominently in art and stories. From festivals to galleries to dozens of museums, historic sites, and interpretive and cultural centres, Yukon's story is brought to life for visitors in a great variety of ways.

A Yukon black bear enjoying summer

Did you know ...

* Rivers in the Yukon (there are 13 of them) flow north rather than east.

* The Yukon lies farthest west than any other part of Canada and shares 1040 km of border with the USA State of Alaska.

* Yukon dance hall queen, Diamond Tooth Gertie, made a fortune 'mining' Stampeders of their hard-won gold nuggets. Her nickname came from the sparkling diamond she had wedged between her two front teeth.

* One of the lowest recorded temperatures in North America was recorded in the western Yukon in 1947. It was -63 °C.

* The long hours of summer sunshine in the North have earned the Yukon the nickname "Land of the Midnight Sun."

* Dawson City was home to the Dawson City Nuggets hockey team, who, in 1905, challenged the Ottawa Senators (aka the Silver Seven) for the Stanley Cup. The team travelled to Ottawa by dogsled, ship, and train. The Dawson City team lost the most lopsided series in Stanley Cup history, losing two games by the combined score of 32 to 4. *(Ouch! But you have to admire their persistence just to* **get** *to Ottawa!)*

* Dog power has been used for hunting and travel for over a thousand years. As far back as the 10th century these dogs have contributed to human culture. They have pulled sleds on snow and different rigs on dry land.

* Assembling a dog sled team involves picking leader dogs, point dogs, swing dogs, and wheel dogs. The lead dog is crucial so mushers take particular care of these dogs. Read more online here:

   yukonquest.com/news/sled-dogs-north

* In recreational dog sledding, Siberian Huskies or Alaskan Malamutes are the main types of dogs used because of their attractive looks and willingness to work. However, Alaskan Huskies are the most popular breed for sled dog *racing*, because of their endurance, speed, and dedication to running even when tired.

* 80% of the Yukon is wilderness area and it provides great habitats for beavers, martens, mink, and arctic and red foxes. You could encounter wolves, otters, coyotes and elk and you might see an enormous moose taking a drink from a bone-chilling lake. *(It's an awesome sight because they are so huge! Just a reminder that you can see great pictures of moose at the video site in the New Brunswick Chapter.)*

* In the Takhini Hot Pools, you could take part in a really unique contest every February. Just photograph yourself with frozen hair in the hot springs. The best picture receives a cash prize and a complimentary pool pass. *(Sounds like fun!)*

Takhini Hot Pools in winter

* The three types of bears common to North America are the American black bear, the grizzly bear and the polar bear, and they are all found in the Yukon.

* A resident of the Yukon is often called a "sourdough," and the name came from the use of sourdough for making bread in prospectors' camps. I don't think he was often called a 'sourdough,' but the American author, Jack London, lived in the Yukon, and it was there he wrote *Call of the Wild*. *(Have you read it? I think young teens might even enjoy it.)*

* Robert W. Service wrote some wonderful poems, yet he is not well known by many Canadians. His poems have interesting names such as *The Shooting of Dan McGrew* and *The Cremation of Sam McGee. (I'm sure you would find them in your local library.)*

* Yukoners love to have fun and that includes having many different races. The dogsled races are very popular, but so also are the bathtub races from Whitehorse to Dawson on the Yukon River, and the annual Great Klondike International Outhouse Race. Anyone can enter and if you didn't bring your own outhouse one is supplied. ☺

Northwest Territories Flower

Mountain Avens

Jane Crosby, 2015, watercolour 20 x 12 cm

14

The Northwest Territories (NWT) – Canada's Last Frontier

Population: 43,537   Joined Confederation: July 15, 1870

City: Yellowknife (Capital – where 19,000 of the population live)

Towns: Hay River, Inuvik, Fort Smith, Norman Wells

Places to Visit/Things to See:

The Northern Lights	Virginia Falls in Nahanni National Park
Panning for Gold	Whooping cranes in Wood Buffalo Natural Park
Caribou Carnival	The Prince of Wales Northern Heritage Centre

History

It seems there have always been more animals than people in the Northwest Territories! Valuable fur-bearing animals such as muskrat and beaver have roamed the area for decades. Also native are moose, wolves, black and grizzly bears, and mountain sheep and goats.

A variety of Aboriginal cultures has been scattered over the land for thousands of years. Since about 1100 they have included the Dene, Inuvialuit (Inuit), and more recently, the Métis. The Inuit are descendants of the *Thule* who migrated eastward from Alaska. In Inuktitut the Northwest Territories is referred to as *Nunatsiaq* meaning "beautiful land." This territory encompasses over one million square kilometres.

Martin Frobisher began the search in 1576 and many other explorers continued it - seeking a Northwest Passage through northern Arctic waters. William Baffin and Henry Hudson in the 1600s and James Cook and Alexander Mackenzie in the 1700s continued searching for this elusive passage to Asia. A Norwegian, Roald Amundsen, was the first explorer to find and navigate the Northwest Passage in 1906. *(You will see on the map many bays, straits and rivers in the north named for these explorers.)*

An interesting story of the Sir John Franklin expedition in **1845** has made exciting news in **2014** an **2016**. Apparently, his two boats disappeared among icebergs and choppy, freezing waters and were never seen again. Many searches throughout the 19th century attempted to find the lost ships, but none was successful until now! Finding Franklin's ship, the *HMS Erebus*, in 2014, in Queen Maud Gulf, had solved one of Canada's greatest mysteries. Finding the *HMS Terror* in 2016 has added to the excitement. Both ships were located with the help of the Inuit. Now, would England claim ownership because the ship embarked from its shores, or will Canada claim it because it is in Canadian waters? To find out more, search for Arctic Research Foundation. You may also find videos of the discovery at cbc.ca

In Inuktituit, the language of the Inuit people, the Northwest Territories is referred to as "beautiful land." Did you think that was 'bad grammar' to say the NWTerritories IS instead of ARE? It would be, except NWT is always referred to as singular not plural. *(I know it is strange, but then so is Newfoundland and Labrador being one province...no comment!)*

The Northwest Territories has the largest population of the three northern territories. Yellowknife, its largest city, became the territorial capital in 1967. There were gold mines in the area and it was big business to supply them all in the 1930s. However, in the 1940s, mining ceased, as men became Canadian troops in World War II.

Just as the railway had opened up the huge expanse of Canada "from sea to sea," the *"bush plane" transformed the north. In 1917-18 bush planes began flying supplies into northern Québec and Ontario; they spotted forest fires and delivered mail. Bush flying to supply mines continued even through the Great Depression. By the 1930s, it became possible to charter an aircraft and fly almost anywhere. Helicopters have been introduced along with better weather information services. However, it's the aircraft equipped with floats or skis that continue to serve all those who live and work in remote areas.

*In Canada the word "bush" has been used since the 19th C to describe the hostile environment beyond the clearings and settlements. In bush flying, it has been used to refer to flying in poor, if not hostile, conditions in the remote areas beyond the ribbon of settlement in southern Canada, into the "bush" of the North and the barren Arctic. *(The bush plane story is online at the Canadian Encyclopedia site, and it makes fascinating reading. Also, you may enjoy watching online "Arctic Air," the television fictional drama series about flying bush planes in the Arctic.)*

**The de Havilland of Canada DHC-2 Beaver
- serving the Canadian north**

Diamonds are still being mined "up north" – over $450 million worth each year. However, it is also sobering to know there is controversy over the effects that 23 mines are having on the natural environment. *(We are trusting the federal government will keep a close watch on environmental changes in the North. The tailings from diamond mines are very toxic not only for the land but also for the people.)*

Through the 1970s and 1980s, there were gold mines, diamond mines and several mines for silver and tungsten in the Northwest Territories. Many have closed down now leaving mostly diamond mines operating. In the Dogrib language, the city of Yellowknife is called Comba K'E which means, "where the money is." *(It seems appropriate these days, considering the number of mines in the area!)*

The Northwest Territories Today

Although the Northwest Territories entered confederation in July 1867, the current borders were formed April 1, 1999, when the territory was subdivided to create Nunavut to the east. Nunavut is Canada's third and newest territory.

The southern part of the NWT territory (most of the mainland portion) has a subarctic climate while the islands and northern coast have a polar climate. The **subarctic climate** is characterized by long, usually very cold winters, and short, cool to mild summers. Regions with a **polar climate** are characterized by a lack of warm summers. Every month in a **polar climate** has an average temperature of less than 10 °C. *(No question why big furry polar bears like the northern climate!)*

Scientists are paying close attention to temperatures rising in northern Canada. If temperatures continue to rise in Arctic regions, many territorial animals will suffer. The numbers of caribou, muskox, seals, sea lions and walruses will decline. Polar bears will suffer the most, as longer ice-free periods will alter their feeding habits. To find out more about the effects on arctic wildlife as sea ice hits an historic low this year, and how you may help to save amazing species like polar bears, go here:

worldwildlife.org

A polar bear realizing his "ice pans" are slowly disappearing

(I was amazed and dismayed to learn that climate change is warming the Arctic at twice the rate of the rest of the planet. Immediate action is needed! Read more in stories at the world wildlife organization and also here: wwf.ca/*).*

Two "gems" in the middle of Yellowknife to visit are the Frame Lake Trail and the Legislative Assembly Building. During summer months, when it's still "bright as day" at midnight, tourists like to take a long "after dinner stroll" around the lake before bedtime. *(At least we did! Have you ever been in a place where it's as light as noon hour at midnight?)*

During the day, tourists may tour the unique Legislative Assembly Building. Set on the shores of Frame Lake, it's designed with themes from local native populations. Lots of natural materials were used - the hand-tooled zinc panel behind the speaker's chair (zinc is mined here), maple wood ceiling, slate floors and many windows to let in natural light. One insightful design is the vent panel in each Member's office for user-control of fresh air. This was thoughtful for native Members who may not be accustomed to spending days in an air-conditioned office building. *(When I toured this building, I was awed by how it seemed to literally "belong" with the trees and shrubs around it. Also amazing, was the translation service available in the 11 official languages of the territory.)*

Northwest Territories Legislative Assembly, Yellowknife

I forgot to say the Chamber and Caucus rooms are circular to support the consensus-style government these Legislative Members model. *(This circular environment would surely make things less "us vs them" than in all our older Legislative Buildings. Most were built on the old British "adversarial model" i.e. two sides facing each other.)*

Great Bear Lake attracts boaters and fishers – during the four months of the year it is not covered with ice! It is the largest lake wholly in Canada (Lake Superior and Lake Huron are larger but they lie partly in the USA). It is the fourth largest lake in North America and the eighth largest in the world. Martens and grizzly bears can be seen in summer and elk walk along the shore in the winter. Great Bear Lake has achieved more angling records than any other lake in North America! It is especially famous for its trout, and some have weighed in at 65 lbs. *(Wow! I'm told an average trout in rivers and lakes on the west coast of Canada might top 20 to 40 lbs. I'm not sure why we use the metric system for most things but not the weight of fish. Maybe you know?)*

The Northwest Territories is about six times the size of the United Kingdom and it has a few more airports, e.g. 68 land airports or water aerodrome landing space and four heliports. *(Not surprising since roads are few and far between!)*

We cannot leave the north without an example of the beautiful native crafts. The artists make lovely soft, beaded moccasins and clothing that require hours of painstaking work. I think this craft tops them all. The artist snips the softer "under hair" from the moose or caribou hide, holds it within a loop of thread then sets it snugly against a garment or material. The artist then delicately snips the hair. The process is repeated until a flower or other pattern springs forth. The hair can be dyed to make the variety of colours. *(Below is a wonderful example of one I almost had. I just have to share the story.)*

(Years ago, I was in Yellowknife at a Public Health silent auction fundraiser, and I bid on one of these beautiful pictures made on black velvet. Just as the auction was closing, I saw someone else making a bid after mine! When she turned around, I was excited to see our kids' favourite babysitter whom I hadn't seen in over 25 years! I was not *as excited that she won the picture...we have never been back to the "north" again...my loss.* ☹*)*

A beautiful moose hair tufting picture

From beautiful mittens made in Newfoundland to the Pysankas of Alberta and gorgeous tufting pictures made in the Northwest Territories, I think we've seen some of Canada's exquisite crafts from the Atlantic to the Arctic!

Did you know ...

* Regions with **polar climate** cover over 20% of the Earth. This means the sun shines 24-hours-a-day in the summer and rarely shines in the winter. The highs in the summertime don't go above 10 °C.

* Aulavik National Park on Banks Island is totally treeless – not even one single tree – but it has the highest concentration of muskoxen on earth. To see them, you'd have to charter an airplane as there are no roads there. *(About 114 people live on the island so you know for sure they have no traffic jams!)*

* In the 1950s, during the darkest, coldest days of winter, a 520 km road made entirely of ice and snow was built to go from Yellowknife to a silver mine above the Arctic Circle. *(We have a friend who drove trucks across this "ice road" for many a long winter. He has many "hair-raising" stories to tell! You might like to check out the CBC television series "Ice Road Truckers" here:* History.com*).*

* These winter routes over frozen lakes and rivers are really dangerous. The truckers haul vital supplies to the mines in remote locations and run the risk of breaking through the ice. When this happens, the driver has less than a minute to get out or he will freeze to death.

* The gyrfalcon is the official NWT territorial bird and white pelicans can be found along the Slave River. Unfortunately, these pelicans are now an endangered species.

* Wood Buffalo National Park lies in northeastern Alberta and southern Northwest Territories. It is the largest park in Canada and the second in the world after Chugach State Park in Anchorage, Alaska.

* The 19,000 residents of Yellowknife celebrate the end of winter with the Caribou Carnival. Activities include dog-sled races, ice carving, ugly truck and dog contests, and snow canoe races. *(Wouldn't it be fun to compare their ice carvings with the ones from Québec's winter carnival, eh?)*

* Because agriculture is almost impossible due to the frozen ground, much fresh food has to be brought in by airplane. Small communities rely heavily on floatplanes.

* The cost of living in the NWT is at least 60% higher than in the rest of Canada, one of the main costs being the price of food.

* Great Slave Lake is the deepest body of water in North America being 614 metres deep.

* Although it was just a prank, it was a bit scary when Nunavut split off from the Northwest Territories in 1999 and some people wanted to rename the NWT "Bob."

* The Northwest Territories is often referred to as being "north of sixty." This is because the north - south boundary that divides it from the provinces of BC, Alberta and Saskatchewan, runs along the 60th parallel.

* Travel, tourism, and cultural education are the fastest growing industries in the territory. Growth is promoted by government in these areas in the hope that people will be encouraged to work and live in the region.

* In 1873, the government of Canada created what is now the Royal Canadian Mounted Police (RCMP) to establish order across the country. In the NWT, they drove out troublesome hunters and trappers and today the RCMP remains the only police force in the territory.

* In the planning stages, the RCMP was originally called the North West Mounted Rifles. They had to change their name when the United States reacted negatively to the idea of armed military patrolling their border!

Have you ever seen this warning sign in your travels? ☺

Nunavut Territory Flower

Purple Saxifrage
Jane Crosby, 2016, watercolour 11 x 18 cm

15

Nunavut (NU) – Canada's Newest Territory

Population: 31,906 in 2011   Joined Confederation: July 1, 1999

Cities: Apex, Baker Lake, Cape Dorset, Eskimo Point, Frobisher, Rankin Inlet, Ward Inlet, Iqaluit (ee-KAL-oo-it) on Baffin Island (Capital)

Towns: Bathurst Inlet, Cambridge Bay, Chesterfield Inlet, Igloolik, Resolute,

Places to Visit/Things to See:

Sylvia Grinnel Territorial Park   The Nunatta Sunakkutaangit Museum
The Legislative Building   Toonik Tyme
Various wildlife tours   Beluga whales sighting

Nunavut is pronounced Noo-na-voot and means "Our Land" in Inukitut.

History

Over 4,000 years ago, it was thought that the Baffin coast was identified in the sagas of explorers from Norway. Two distinct but physically related groups of indigenous people have inhabited this Arctic area – one group for over 4000 years and the other for 1000 years. Between 1500 and 1000 years ago, some Inuit groups learned to hunt the large bowhead whales in the arctic seas. Large communities were created along the northern coast of Alaska, then some of these North Alaska Inuit spread quickly eastwards across arctic Canada and Greenland. *(See the Inuit Range Map above.)*

These early Inuit, called Thule people, brought with them their kayaks with throwing-harpoons attached to floats; equipment for hunting and travelling on the ice; bows for hunting on land, and insulated winter boulder and turf houses. They traded with the Norsemen for metal tools.

In the 1500s, Inuit culture changed significantly. Most regions of the High Arctic and whaling were abandoned. Groups began to hunt smaller sea mammals, caribou and fish. But they could not get enough food to survive the winter if they stayed in one place. They began to winter in snow-house communities so they could hunt seals through the ice.

Inuit village of snow-houses in 1575

Recorded history began in 1576 when Martin Frobisher sailed from England looking for the Northwest Passage to China (then known as Cathay). He made three voyages and named Frobisher Bay but he couldn't find the fabled Northwest Passage. In 1610, Henry Hudson also came from England searching unsuccessfully for the Northwest Passage. *(I guess they just weren't meant to find that passage!)*

Changes in Inuit culture may have been caused by the climate cooling down making the traditional Thule economy impossible. More European fishermen, explorers, whalers and traders arrived, and along with missionaries greatly influenced the traditional Inuit ways of life. The fur trade became very important as whaling declined. These intruders brought with them guns, cloth, metal tools, and utensils, and even musical instruments. They also brought alcohol and tobacco, disease and new genes. The ancient history of Nunavut and of the Inuit involves great movements of populations, and marvelous achievements.

The present day Inuit are descendants of these groups. They tell stories of the "qallunaat" (outsiders) – whalers, fur traders, and other "seekers" – who came to use the resources but not to settle in the area.

Nunavut means "our land" in Inuktitut. A "summer carpet of colour" where caribou roam freely.

In the 19th century, the written histories showed the contrast between the Inuit and the Europeans who arrived on Inuit land. The Inuit had long ago adapted well to their harsh environment, and many times they helped the newcomers as guides, hunters and interpreters. Many "seekers" owed their lives to the wisdom of the Inuit. *(I hope written history shows that these "seekers" were grateful to the Inuit people.)*

By about 1920, most exploration was over, and few bowhead whales remained in arctic waters. The Canadian Government was concerned by the presence of American whalers and foreign explorers in the High Arctic. The **N**orth **W**est **M**ounted **P**olice arrived and set up and posts to enforce Canadian law and to exert control in the area.

The first explorer to find the Northwest Passage was the Norwegian, Roald Amundsen during his expeditions in 1903-1906. For the next 100 years it couldn't be used as a regular shipping route for the large ships because of the Arctic pack ice. However, recent changes in the ice caused by climate change have made the route more navigable. *(In fact, I have just seen a picture of the first cruise ship to go through that passage. I imagine it will be the first of many. People are concerned that this increased 'tourism' will negatively affect the habitats of the animals in these waters. What do you think of tourism in Arctic waters?)*

The Inuit forefathers were expert kayak makers. They made the kayak with animal skins stretched over frames of driftwood or bone. The Inuit say that the canoe was made long before the kayak, and carbon dating agrees. Originally, they were made from dugout tree trunks, birch bark and other lightweight watertight materials. One recovered example of a canoe has been carbon dated to 8000 BC. *(Our family's canoe is a polymer or something dating back to the 1970s but it still floats! I especially like the little 1.5 hp motor that gets us home when we are too tired to paddle anymore!)*

Paddling kayaks and canoes in the frigid Arctic waters was not without its hazards. As sturdy as the little crafts were, the hunters would stay away from large groups of animals that could capsize them, such as a group of walruses. However, from their kayaks, the Inuit were amazing hunters of whales and seals.

The beach seems a bit crowded today!

In 1880, the Arctic Islands were transferred from Britain to Canada. Several "official expeditions" visited the High Arctic in the early 1900s. This was to exert Canadian sovereignty and collect Customs fees from whalers. Future shipping through the region will be interesting not only because the Canadian government considers the area part of Canada, but also because the USA and Europe consider the area a public shipping lane. Much discussion will probably continue! However, some parts of the waterways are only 4.5 metres deep so large vessels could not get through.

The Second World War and the Cold War opened the Canadian Arctic. The United States Air Force built an airfield at Frobisher Bay (now Iqaluit) to fly war materials to Europe. In 1957, the Distant Early Warning (DEW) Line, a joint project of Canada and the United States was completed. This was an early-warning radar chain that was intended to warn of any Soviet invasions. It was upgraded in the 1980s, renamed the North Warning System, and sole management was given to Canada.

Nunavut Today

Iqaluit, the capital city of Nunavut, is situated on Baffin Island. Its 6,699 residents are living about 2000 km north of Ottawa, the capital of Canada. *(That's about the same distance that Vancouver, British Columbia, is west of Ottawa, Ontario.)*

The late 1960s was a time of "re-imagining" of the Arctic by a group of visionary "Eskimos." They began their political movement by challenging the use of the word Eskimo. In the Arctic of the 1970s, an Inuit non-profit association was founded to represent the Inuit living in the four regions of Canada. Their study of Inuit history and land use showed the extent of Inuit Aboriginal title in the Arctic.

In **1976** the association proposed to settle the Inuit land claims by creating the territory of Nunavut. It would be carved from the eastern part of the Northwest Territories. It led to the largest land claim in western civilization - all organized by young visionary Inuit with a dream - governance of their own territory. Governments are notoriously slow to act *(as we all know!)* and to get all the "agreements" in place took until April 1, **1999** to create Nunavut. There were no riots, no demonstrations, and no violence as that is not the Inuit culture. They went to Ottawa year after year to negotiate their land claims and they won the peaceful "Inuit way." *(This is one reason I am proud to be a Canadian. I loved to see the Inuit reach their dreams! See the amazing film Arctic Defenders. You may find it in your public library.)*

It has been a "western fad" for years for mothers to carry their infants in "snuggies" or front packs. Mothers in Nunavut carry their infant children in the hood of their 'amauti' — a specially designed Inuit parka. To survive in the harsh arctic, Inuit men mastered the design of specialized hunting tools. The Inuit women mastered all the local materials and forms of their traditional clothing. Parkas and sealskin boots are still beautifully handmade in Nunavut. Inuit art is alive and well in the incredible Inuit beadwork patterns, plus intricately worked bone, stone, talon, claw, ivory and metal jewellery.

Tourism is slowly growing during the summer season and territorial parks and adventure activities are available. The number one priority for the

Inuit is preservation of their land and wildlife. Many parks, wildlife areas and bird sanctuaries are protected. Tourists must register to hike in most parks and must first watch an orientation video to become familiar with hiking on land that may not always be solid! *(This sounds like "adventure hiking" at its best!)*

Did you know ...

* In the Nunavut flag, the colours blue and gold stand for the richness of the land, sea and sky. The red stands for Canada and the inuksuk represents the stone monuments created to mark special places and to guide people through the Arctic. The blue star is the North Star, which also helps guide people. It also represents the guidance of the elders, which remains unchanged like the star.

* The inuksuk is a man-made stone landmark used by native people in the Arctic area where there are few natural landmarks. It may have been used for navigation or to mark routes to special places such as good hunting areas.

* At Enukso Point on Baffin Island, there are over 100 inuksuit. The site was designated a National Historic Site of Canada in 1969. The size of some inuksuit suggests groups made them. (Inuksuit is the plural of inukshuk.)

> You may see a quick video clip explaining the inuksuk here:
> wn.com/inukshuk

* If Nunavut were a country, it would be the 15th largest in the world – larger than Mexico.

* Nunavut is actually a polar desert and not covered in snow. It gets less than 250 millimeters of snow per year. *(Amazing! I always thought the "far north" was all just "snow and ice"!)*

* The town of Alert is 817.5 km from the North Pole and 1834.6 km north of the Arctic Circle. It is the northernmost settlement in the world. *(I wonder if anyone ever sees Santa Claus up there! ☺)*

The Whistler Mountain Inukshuk, created as a symbol of the 2010 Winter Olympic Games, has become an unofficial symbol of Canada.

* "Operation Boxtop" is an air resupply mission that's flown every April and September to the Canadian Forces Station in Alert. The large Hercules transport planes fly dry goods and fuel critical to the continued mission of Canadian allies at these austere locations. The crash of a "Boxtop" plane in October 1991, was the subject of several books as well as a film *Ordeal in the Arctic* starring Richard Chamberlain.

* The petals of the territorial flower, the purple saxifrage, are slightly sticky and they can be eaten. At first they taste bitter but after a few seconds they become sweet. They also contain vitamin C. *(Oranges would be rare — and expensive — in the Arctic so it's good the flower contains vitamin C!)*

* The purple saxifrage is found throughout the arctic and bloom after the snow melts. They are very hardy and can grow in gravel and very poor soil. The Inuit know that when the plant blooms, the caribou herds are calving. *(That plant makes a good calendar!)*

* The Nunatta Sunakkutaangit Museum in Iqaluit, provides visitors with an historical perspective on Inuit culture. It includes Inuit artifacts and galleries showing works of local artists. The past and present of Arctic society meet here.

* Baffin Island is the largest island in Canada and the fifth largest island in the world. It has huge areas of land that slope into plateaus still covered in ice year-round. Its many freshwater lakes and rivers thaw only for a short time in the brief Arctic summer.

* In February 2010, Iqaluit hosted the meeting of the G7 finance ministers - an economic and political group of the world's seven largest industrialized nations. The unique skills of Native Throat Singers and Drum Dancers entertained them.

* Visitors like to try Ice Golfing, not on "greens" but on "whites." They would play on an 18-hole ice golf course in the bay near Iqaluit where they would play not with golf balls because they freeze in extreme cold, but with brightly coloured tennis balls instead.

* The unspoiled land and sea of the Arctic region is also home to one of nature's most magnificent landscapes; the "floe edge" from April to July. The "floe edge" is where the sea meets the retreating ice edge, and where whales swim just metres from shore. Walruses and seals haul themselves out of the sea to bask in the sun, and massive icebergs float slowly by.

* When the ice is melting on the ice golf course, you can always join "Toonik Tyme." This is a spring festival held in most communities consisting of Inuit sports, music, sled races, ice carving and igloo carving.

I am a beluga whale swimming in Cunningham Inlet.

16

Grammar Excercises

Canada

PRACTICE with NOUNS

Nouns are the names of persons, places or things. The names of *people* are usually capitalized (singer kd lang is an exception) and the names of *cities* and *countries* begin with a capital letter as well. Most *things* are not capitalized – unless they begin a sentence. The subject of a sentence is the person/thing that does the action. For example:

Pierre Berton wrote many books.

Pierre Berton is the subject of the action word (verb) 'wrote'.

Now it's your turn to find, underline and correct all the nouns in the following sentences.

1. ottawa is the capital city of canada, but toronto is the capital of ontario.

2. The book *the last spike* was written by the famous canadian author, pierre berton. berton wrote great non-fiction books about canadian history. The book I especially like to give to my American family is called *why we act like canadians*.

3. have you visited halifax or dartmouth? They are cities in nova scotia.

4. Many place names in Canada come from Aboriginal Bands that are Canada's first settlers. Many are difficult to pronounce... places such as musquodoboit, kenebecasis, nauwigewauk or uculet, and assinaboine! *(I'm glad I don't have to learn to spell them! Spell Check makes it easier, however, I've found they are not all in Spell Check!)*

5. Have you heard of the canadian singers anne murray, and shania twain or gordon lightfoot, and céline dion?

6. hockey is a game most canadians love to watch – or play! many famous hockey players on both canadian and american national hockey teams are canadians.

7. the world's first all-girl quintuplets to survive birth were born may 28, 1934 in a small farmhouse in northern ontario. their combined weight was about six kilograms.

8. canada's national anthem, *O Canada,* was first performed on june 24, 1880 during St. jean baptiste day celebrations in Québec city. twenty-eight years later it was translated into english. Finally, agreeing to a few alterations, parliament adopted it as canada's national anthem in 1967. *(It took so long, it's a wonder everyone remembered the tune!)*

9. do try to visit regina, saskatchewan, in 2067 and watch the opening of a time capsule buried in 1967 in a cairn there. The time capsule celebrated 100 years of confederation and will be opened on canada's 200th anniversary. *(It would be fun to read a newspaper from 1967!)*
cairn =a man-made container, in this case made of stone, concrete or some other non-perishable substance

10. david suzuki is a "canadian icon," an internationally famous geneticist and environmental activist. The author of 52 books and several television series in which he made science fascinating, he has helped generations know the importance of caring for our planet.

For extra practice, can you <u>double underline</u> the nouns that are the <u>subject</u> of each sentence?

Answers on next page

1. <u>Ottawa</u> is the capital <u>city</u> of <u>Canada</u>, but <u>Toronto</u> is the <u>capital</u> of <u>Ontario</u>.

2. The <u>book</u> *The Last Spike* was written by the famous Canadian <u>author</u>, Pierre <u>Berton</u>. <u>Berton</u> wrote great non-fiction <u>books</u> about Canadian history. The <u>book</u> I especially like to give to my American <u>family</u> is called *Why We Act Like Canadians*.

3. Have you visited <u>Halifax</u> or <u>Dartmouth</u>? These <u>cities</u> are in <u>Nova Scotia</u>.

4. Many place <u>names</u> in <u>Canada</u> come from Aboriginal <u>Bands</u> that are Canada's first <u>settlers</u>. Many are difficult to pronounce… <u>places</u> such as <u>Musquodoboit</u>, <u>Kenebecasis</u>, <u>Nauwigewauk</u>, <u>Uculet</u>, and Assinaboine! *(I'm glad I didn't have to learn to spell them! But today it's easy with Spell Check! However, I've found that they are not all in Spell Check!)*

5. Have you heard of the Canadian <u>singers</u> <u>Anne Murray</u>, and <u>Shania Twain</u> or <u>Gordon</u> <u>Lightfoot</u>, and <u>Céline Dion</u>?

6. <u>Hockey</u> is a game most <u>Canadians</u> love to watch – or play! Many famous hockey <u>players</u> on both Canadian and American national hockey teams are <u>Canadians</u>.

7. The world's first all-girl <u>quintuplets</u> to survive birth were born May 28, 1934 in a small <u>farmhouse</u> in northern <u>Ontario</u>. Their combined <u>weight</u> was about six <u>kilograms</u>.

8. Canada's national <u>anthem</u>, *O Canada,* was first performed on <u>June</u> 24, 1880 during <u>Saint</u> <u>Jean</u> <u>Baptiste</u> <u>Day</u> celebrations in <u>Québec City</u>. Twenty-eight <u>years</u> later it was translated into <u>English</u>. Finally, agreeing to a few <u>alterations</u>, <u>Parliament</u> (the Federal Government) adopted it as Canada's national <u>anthem</u> in 1967. *(It took so long it's a wonder everyone remembered the tune!)*

9. Do try to visit <u>Regina</u>, <u>Saskatchewan</u> in 2067 and watch the opening of a time <u>capsule</u> buried in a <u>cairn</u> there in 1967. It celebrated 100 <u>years</u> of <u>Confederation</u> and will be opened on Canada's 200th <u>anniversary</u>. *(It would be fun to read a newspaper from 1967!)*

*cairn =a man-made container, in this case made of stone, concrete or some other non-perishable substance

10. David Suzuki is a "Canadian icon," an internationally famous geneticist and environmental activist. The author of 52 books and several television series in which he made science fascinating, he has helped generations know the importance of caring for our planet.

PRACTICE with PRONOUNS

A pronoun is a word that can be used to take the place of a noun.
In the sentence *"Sir John A. MacDonald was the first Prime Minister of Canada and he lived in Ottawa,"* the pronoun *he* takes the place of the noun, Sir John A. MacDonald.

There are 3 types of Pronouns: Subject, Object, and Possessive

To keep things simple, let's not use the 12 rules for pronouns! Maybe just 3 will do here!

Rule 1: Subject pronouns are used when the pronoun is the **subject** – or **doer** of the action in the sentence.

> **He** had fun visiting Tuktoyaktuk in the Northwest Territories.
> *They* flew over the Arctic Ocean and saw caribou and reindeer.
> Jan and I loved the Rocky Mountains! *We* are going back to BC soon!

Rule 2: Object pronouns are used almost everywhere else beyond Rule 1.

> Think of subject pronouns as the **doer** of an action.
> Think of object pronouns as the **receiver** of an action.

> The Polar Bear on that ice floe seemed to be headed straight for *them*!
> It seemed to *him*, that the grey wolf stared right into his eyes.
> The fox fur he gave *me* was very soft and silky.

<u>A Note to Remember</u>: Never combine a subject pronoun and an object pronoun in phrases like "her and I" or "he and me". One of the pronouns will always be wrong.

Incorrect: Her and I saw brown bears in the Bella Coola Valley in BC.
Correct: *She* and I saw brown bears…. (you would never say "her saw")

Incorrect: Him and I watched Polar Bear cubs frolicking in the snow.
Correct: *He* and I watched Polar Bear cubs….(you would never say "him watched")

Rule 3: Possessive pronouns are used to refer to a thing or things that belong to a person or people.

> My heart skipped a beat when I saw the grizzly bear! Did *yours*? (your heart)
> After the hike on the glacier, my feet were frozen but *theirs* were not! (their feet)

A very common mistake is to use **it's** - meaning 'it is' – for the possessive pronoun *its.*

Incorrect: The Canadian Beaver uses it's tail to slap the water when danger is near.
Correct: The Canadian Beaver uses *its* tail … (because it's always means it is)

<u>One last note to remember</u>!

Never use the pronouns that end in –self as subjective pronouns. (They are reflexive.)

Incorrect: Joe and *myself* went on the tour of Denali Park in the Yukon.
Correct: Joe and *I* went on the tour….
Correct: I, *myself*, wanted to go on that tour!
Just remember not to use *myself* unless the pronoun **I** <u>comes before</u> it.

Incorrect: My brother and myself rode the gondola at Whistler Mountain in BC.
Correct: My brother and *I* rode the gondola….

Incorrect: Please give the map of Juneau, Alaska, to John and *myself*.

Correct: Please give the map…to John and *me*. (me is the objective pronoun/receiver)

Now it's your turn to choose the correct pronoun in the following sentences - remembering the 3 rules and the 'note' about reflexive pronouns.

1. Canada did not receive (it's, its) own flag until February 1965.

2. Canada's first inhabitants were many Bands of Aboriginal peoples. (Canada, It) owed (its, it's) growth to many waves of immigrants from Europe and the British Isles.

3. (Her, She) and I enjoyed a trip through the Gastown area of Vancouver.

4. If (you and her)(you and she) want to see real dinosaur bones, visit Alberta!

5. My brother and (myself, I, me) toured the beautiful "old town" area of Québec City.

6. Raccoons are becoming a nuisance in many Canadian cities. (Raccoons, They) have learned how to cooperate to push over garbage cans and feast on the contents!

7. Logging is an industry in many Canadian provinces, and statistics show which province depends on (logging, it) to boost (their, its) economy. For example, you will find 1,012 logging companies in British Columbia and 38 logging companies in Saskatchewan.

Let's make these ones a bit more challenging! You supply a relevant pronoun for the underlined nouns.

8. The hearts of many people around the world continue to beat due to the invention of Manitoba-born, William Bigelow. William Bigelow invented the pacemaker.

9. Russia is the largest, but with 3,855,103 square miles, Canada is the second largest country in the world, and <u>Canada</u> has similar uninhabited areas of ice and snow.

10. Alert, in Nunavut Territory, is the northernmost permanent settlement in the world but most of <u>Alert's</u> residents live temporarily in weather and military groups.

* **Q:** Do you know how to tell if a person is a Canadian?

Answers on next page

Note the correct pronouns in the following sentences:

1. Canada did not receive **its** own flag until February 1965.

2. Canada's first inhabitants were many Bands of Aboriginal peoples. Canada owed **its** growth to many waves of immigrants from Europe and the British Isles.

3. **She** and I enjoyed a trip through the Gastown area of Vancouver.

4. If **you and she** want to see real dinosaur bones, visit Alberta!

5. My brother and **I** toured the beautiful "old town" area of Québec City.

6. Raccoons are becoming a nuisance in many Canadian cities. **They** have learned how to cooperate to push over garbage cans and feast on the contents!

7. Logging is an industry in many Canadian provinces, and statistics show which province depends on **it** to boost **its** economy. For example, you will find 1,012 logging companies in British Columbia and 38 logging companies in Saskatchewan.

Have you supplied these pronouns for the following 3 sentences?

8. The hearts of many people around the world continue to beat due to the invention of Manitoba-born, William Bigelow. **He** invented the pacemaker. *(My husband's pacemaker keeps his heart beating well, and he is still with us today, thanks to Mr. Bigelow.)*

9. Russia is the largest, but at 3,855,103 square miles, Canada is the second largest country in the world, and **it** has similar uninhabited areas of ice and snow.

10. Alert, in Nunavut Territory, is the northernmost permanent settlement in the world but most of **its** residents live temporarily in weather and military groups.

* A. You can tell someone is a Canadian if they wear a toque, use hockey tape to fix everything and say "eh" a lot!

Newfoundland

MORE PRACTICE with NOUNS and PRONOUNS

Nouns are the names of persons, places or things. The names of *people* are usually capitalized (singer kd lang is an exception!) and the names of *cities* and *countries* begin with a capital letter as well. Most *things* are not capitalized – unless they begin a sentence.

Pronouns take the place of nouns. Use *who* to refer to people; and *what, which* or *that* to refer to places and things. When first learning English it is ok to think of *which* and *that* as equal, i.e. you may use either.

Now it's your turn to underline the nouns and choose the proper pronouns in the following sentences.

1. The easternmost spot in Canada is Cape Spear, (that, which) is in Newfoundland.

2. The Bay of Bulls is a great place to find the puffins – sometimes called sea parrots - (who, that) are Newfoundland's provincial bird.

3. The "Screech In" event (that, who) makes you an honorary Newfoundlander means that you must kiss a cod fish – sort of!

4. St. John's is the capital city of Newfoundland, not to be confused with Saint John (who, which, that) is a city in the province of New Brunswick.

5. Newfoundlanders pick yummy berries, called bakeapples (which, who) are very hard to pick because (it, they) grow very far apart in bogs! *(Salmon berries are much easier to pick!)*

6. You would enjoy seeing the crafts in the wee shop in St. Anthony – and you might even see huge icebergs (who, which) drift into the harbour.

7. People (that, who) live in Newfoundland don't have to fear snakes, or poison ivy because there is neither in the province!

8. The Canadian cities (who, that) have the cloudiest, rainiest and windiest weather, are all in Newfoundland. Fog creeps along (its, their) shores about 124 days each year.

9. There were no squirrels in Newfoundland until 1963. Scientists, (that, who) thought they were being helpful, introduced them! *(Helpful? Ha! Newfoundlanders say they are cute but an awful nuisance!)*

10. Gros Morne National Park is a UNESCO World Heritage site. (Her, Its) name comes from the high spot, "Gros Morne" ("great somber") Peak. You will find waterfalls and even sea caves there (who, that) will take your breath away!

Answers on next page

In the following sentences, the nouns have been underlined, and the proper pronouns have been selected.

1. The easternmost spot in Canada is Cape Spear, **which** is in Newfoundland.

2. The Bay of Bulls is a great place to find the puffins – sometimes called sea parrots - **that** are Newfoundland's provincial bird.

3. The "Screech In" event **that** makes you an honorary Newfoundlander means that you must kiss a cod fish – sort of!

4. St. John's is the capital city of Newfoundland, not to be confused with Saint John **which** or **that** is a city in the Province of New Brunswick.

5. Newfoundlanders pick yummy berries, called bakeapples **which** take a long time to pick because **they** grow very far apart in bogs!

6. You would enjoy seeing the crafts in the wee shop in St. Anthony – and you might even see huge icebergs **that** drift into the harbour.

7. People **who** live in Newfoundland don't have to fear snakes, or poison ivy because there is neither in the province!

8. The Canadian cities **that** have the cloudiest, rainiest and windiest weather are all in Newfoundland. Fog creeps along **its** shores about 124 days each year.

9. There were no squirrels in Newfoundland until 1963. Scientists, **who** thought they were being helpful, introduced them! *(Helpful? Ha! Newfoundlanders say squirrels are cute but an awful nuisance!)*

10. Gros Morne National Park is a UNESCO World Heritage site. **Its** name comes from the high spot, "Gros Morne" ("great somber") Peak. You will find fjords, waterfalls and even sea caves there **that** will take your breath away!

The Maritimes

PRACTICE with VERBS – really easy ones!

Let's explore some examples of verbs – action words that make our sentences interesting. It does take some memorizing to use the tense of verbs correctly, so let's just use some simple examples here.

To speak about an action happening *now*, you use the *present* tense of a verb.

I <u>see</u> you studying about Peggy's Cove, Nova Scotia.

You <u>know</u> the explanation of Magnetic Hill in New Brunswick, don't you?

It's legal for drivers <u>to sleep</u> on some parts of the Trans Canada Highway, for example: they <u>sleep</u> on the ferry ride from Wood Islands, Prince Edward Island, to Caribou, Nova Scotia.

To speak about an action that occurred in the *past*, you use the *past tense* of a verb.

I <u>saw</u> you last week at the Anne of Green Gables house in Prince Edward Island.

You <u>learned</u> that the tall ship The *Bluenose* <u>was built</u> in Nova Scotia.

The dessert <u>contained</u> yummy blueberries we <u>picked</u> near Shediac, New Brunswick.

To speak about an action that will happen in the *future*, you use the *future tense*.

I <u>will meet</u> you in the Peggy's Cove gift shop; then we <u>will go</u> whale watching.

He <u>is going</u> to remember <u>driving</u> the long Confederation Bridge from New Brunswick to Prince Edward Island.

Tomorrow she <u>will compare</u> the cities of Saint John, New Brunswick and St. John's, Newfoundland.

To speak about an action that might happen – but it's not certain that it will - you would use the *conditional tense*.

Do you think she <u>would like</u> to take the ferry to Halifax?

He <u>may visit</u> the Annapolis Valley and if he has time, he <u>could pick</u> apples there.

<u>Might it be possible</u> today to visit the Reversing Falls in Saint John, New Brunswick?

Now it's your turn to make a list of the verbs in the following sentences. Label each with a Pr if the verb is in the present tense; a Pa if it's in the past tense, an F if it's in the future tense and a C if it's conditional.

The first one has been done for you.

1. Each of the Maritime Provinces <u>has </u>its own distinctive tartan with rich, interwoven colours. Early settlers in NS probably <u>had</u> their own tartans that <u>indicated</u> their Scottish clan. Every province (except Nunavut) <u>has created</u> a tartan <u>to reflect</u> their specific region of the country.

Verbs: *has* – Pr   *had* – Pa   *indicated* – Pa   *has created* – Pr * to reflect - I

2. Winters in the Maritimes are cold and snowy, so usually you will wear a toque! The word "toque" is a French alteration of "toca" to describe a sailor's cap with a long top.

3. Fort Louisbourg, Nova Scotia is the site of the final battle between the established French and the incoming English. Today, this restored fort shows tourists how people lived in 1774. You will need to respond in French when asked "Qui va la?" (Who goes there?)

4. At Magnetic Hill, just outside Moncton, New Brunswick, excited tourists watch cars roll back up a hill they had just descended – with no help from the astonished driver!

5. When you visit Nova Scotia, you could buy a treat of tasty scallops that come from Digby. You will also see in Maritime grocery stores the delicious McCain Fries made from Prince Edward Island potatoes.

6. My family always enjoyed the potatoes that came from the red earth of PEI. As a child, I usually ate them baked or mashed not as "French fries." It's interesting that there is an ongoing dispute between Belgium and France about which country actually first created "French Fries. " *(Which country do you think created them? Do you like the regular fries or yam fries)*

7. The strong tides of the Bay of Fundy are the largest of all the world's tides. This bay lies between New Brunswick and Nova Scotia and will be a famous tourist attraction for many years to come.

8. The Acadians were a fun-loving and free-spirited people, but in 1775 they were forced from their Maritime homes by the English. This expulsion is a sad event to read about in the pages of Maritime history – but interesting how it influenced Louisiana, USA.

9. A well-loved Acadian writer, Antonine Maillett, from Bouctouche, New Brunswick, is famous for her play *La Sagouine* about a typical Acadian woman. I think you would enjoy meeting her on YouTube. *(I "met" her when I visited Bouctouche! Such fun!)*

10. There are many artists who continue to live and work in the Maritimes. You may do an Internet search for them by just searching for Maritime artists.

Something extra:

* The **Infinitive Form** of the verb is the present tense with a "to" in front of it.

Check back through the previous sentences, find the verbs in the Infinitive form, and double underline them.

You could learn more about the Infinitive verb form if you go here:

Grammar-monster.com/glossary/infinitive_form.htm

Answers on next page

In the following sentences, the verbs have been listed and labeled with the proper tense.

1. Each of the Maritime Provinces has its own distinctive tartan with rich, interwoven colours. Early settlers in NS probably had their own tartans that indicated their Scottish clan. Every province (except Nunavut) has created a tartan to reflect their specific region of the country

Verbs: *has* – Pr   *had* – Pa   *indicated* – Pa   *has created* – Pr

2. Winters in the Maritimes are cold and snowy, so usually you will wear a toque! The word "toque" is a French alteration of "toca" to describe a sailor's cap with a long top.

Verbs: *are* – Pr   *will wear* – F   *is* – Pr

3. Fort Louisbourg, Nova Scotia is the site of the final battle between the established French and the incoming English. Today, this restored fort shows tourists how people lived in 1774. You will need to respond in French when asked "Qui va la?" (Who goes there?)

Verbs: *is* – Pr   *shows* – Pr   *lived* – Pa   *will need* – F   *asked* – Pa   *goes* - Pr

4. At Magnetic Hill, just outside Moncton, New Brunswick, excited tourists watch cars roll back up a hill they had just descended – with no help from the astonished driver!

Verbs: *watch* – Pr   *roll* – Pr   *descended* – Pa

5. When you visit Nova Scotia, you could buy a treat of tasty scallops that come from Digby. You will also see in Maritime grocery stores the delicious McCain Fries made from Prince Edward Island potatoes.

Verbs: *visit* – C   *could buy* – C   *come* – Pr   *will see* – F   *made* – Pa

6. My family always enjoyed the potatoes that came from the red earth of PEI. As a child, I usually ate them baked or mashed not as "French fries." It's interesting that there is an ongoing dispute between Belgium and France about which country actually first created "French Fries." *(Which country do you think created them? Do you like the regular fries or yam fries?)*

Verbs: *enjoyed – Pa   came – Pa   ate – Pa   it's – Pr   is – Pr   created - Pa*

7. The strong tides of the Bay of Fundy are the largest of all the world's tides. This bay lies between New Brunswick and Nova Scotia and will be a famous tourist attraction for many years <u>to come</u>.

Verbs: *are – Pr   lies – Pr   will be – F*

8. The Acadians were a fun-loving and free-spirited people, but in 1775 they were forced from their Maritime homes by the English. This expulsion is a sad event <u>to read</u> about in the pages of Maritime history – but interesting how it influenced Louisiana, USA.

Verbs: *were – Pa   were forced – Pa   is – Pr   influenced - Pa*

9. A well-loved Acadian writer, Antonine Maillett, from Bouctouche, New Brunswick, is famous for her play "La Sagouine" about a typical Acadian woman. I think you would enjoy meeting her on YouTube. *(I "met" her when I visited Bouctouche! Such fun!)*

Verbs: *is – Pr   think – Pr   would enjoy – C   meeting - P*

10. There are many artists who continue <u>to live</u> and work in the Maritimes. You may do an Internet search for them by just searching for Maritime artists.

Verbs: *are – Pr   continue – Pr   work – Pr   may do – C   searching - Pr*

Something extra:

* The **Infinitive Form** of the verb is the present tense with a "to" in front of it.

How many did you find and double underline?

New Brunswick

PRACTICE with VERBS – a variety of verbs

Verbs are action words that make our sentences interesting. As in any language, it does take some memorizing to use the tense of verbs correctly, so let's use some simple examples below. For more complete information about verbs go here:

www.perfect-english-grammar.com/verb-tenses.html

To speak about an action in the <u>present time</u>, you would use the *present tense* of a verb.
I <u>see</u> you reading about the New Brunswick poet, Sir Charles G. D. Roberts.
Do you <u>know</u> the University of New Brunswick <u>is</u> the oldest English University in Canada?
We like <u>to skate</u> on the St. John River because it <u>is</u> amazingly exhilarating!

To speak about an action that occurred in the past, you would use the *past tense* of a verb.
I <u>saw</u> you studying "up the hill" in the university library.
You <u>learned</u> that UNB has a campus in Fredericton and also one in Saint John.
I <u>did not want</u> to visit Fundy National Park this week, I <u>preferred</u> to go to Shediac.

To speak about an action that will happen in the future, you would use the *future tense.*
I <u>will meet</u> you at Tim Horton's in Sackville tomorrow afternoon.
We <u>will enjoy</u> lobster rolls for lunch and <u>we'll sit</u> outside at the Petit Café.

To speak about an action that might happen – but you're not sure it will – you would use the *conditional tense.*
We <u>could go</u> whale watching or we <u>might go</u> kayaking on the Bay of Fundy.
Perhaps she <u>might not like</u> taking long hikes in the NB woods.

Now it's your turn! Make a list of verbs and label them with the proper tense.

Put a Pr if the verb is in the present tense, a Pa if it's in the past tense, an F if it's in the future tense and a C if it's in the conditional tense.

1. Did you know that over 80% of NB is covered with trees?

2. Moosehead Brewery, in Saint John, is Canada's oldest independent brewery.

3. The word "toque" – in Canada – means a knit cap, originally of wool but now often made in synthetic fibres. It always provided warmth in cold weather. Many variations exist all over the world where climate demands a warm hat.

4. Going to and from elementary school in Moncton, I remember hiding behind snow-banks that were way over my head!

5. Many schools in NB had outdoor ice rinks. It was fun to sit with friends in the little wooden "shack" to put on our skates. We would skate until our toes 'froze' and then pop back into the shack to "thaw out" so we could walk home.

6. I would like to see the Hopewell Rocks but I am not sure when the tide will be out so I might be able to get close to these monoliths to take pictures.

7. Do you think she would like to pick blueberries with us? Apparently, NB is well known for yummy-tasting wild ones that grow on small bushes close to the ground.

8. The Bay of Fundy is home to many types of sharks including threshers, makos, porbeagles, and believe it or not, even the Great White Shark has been spotted there.

9. A chocolate museum in St. Stephen houses the original Ganong factory. The Ganongs are Canada's oldest family-owned candy maker and the first to introduce the five cent chocolate bar. *(That must have been quite a few years ago!)*

10. Actor and movie star, Donald Sutherland, father of the TV series "24" star Keifer Sutherland, was introduced to the theatre through puppet classes at the New Brunswick museum in Saint John.

Something extra:

The Infinitive form of the verb is the present tense with a "to" in front of it.

Check back through the previous sentences and see how many verbs in the Infinitive form you can find.

Answers on next page

The verbs have been listed under each sentence and labeled with the proper tense.

Something extra:

The Infinitive form of the verb has been double underlined.

1. Did you know that over 80% of NB is covered with trees?

Verbs: *did know* – Pa   *is covered* – Pr

2. Moosehead Brewery, in Saint John, is Canada's oldest independent brewery.

Verbs: *is* – Pr

3. The word "toque" – in Canada – means a knit cap, originally of wool but now often made in synthetic fibres. It always provided warmth in cold weather. Many variations exist all over the world where climate demands a warm hat.

Verbs: *means* – Pr   *made* – Pr   *provided* – P   *exist* – Pr   *demands* - Pr

4. Going to and from elementary school in Moncton, I remember hiding behind snow-banks that were way over my head!

Verbs: *going* – Pr   *remember* – Pa   *hiding* – Pr   *were* - Pa

5. Many schools in NB had outdoor ice rinks. It was fun to sit with friends in the little wooden "shack" to put on our skates. We would skate until our toes 'froze' and then pop back into the shack to "thaw out" so we could walk home.

Verbs: *had* – Pa   *was* – Pa   *would skate* – C   *pop* – Pr   *could walk* - C

6. I would like to see the Hopewell Rocks but I am not sure when the tide will be out so I might be able to get close to these monoliths to take pictures.

Verbs: *would like* – C   *am not sure* – Pr   *will be out* – F   *might be able* - C

7. Do you think she would like <u>to pick</u> blueberries with us? Apparently, NB is well known for yummy-tasting wild ones that grow on small bushes close to the ground.

Verbs: *think* – Pr   *would like* – C   *is* – Pr   *grow* - Pr

8. The Bay of Fundy is home to many types of sharks including threshers, makos, porbeagles, and believe it or not, even the Great White Shark has been spotted there.

Verbs: *is* – Pr   *believe* – Pr   *has been spotted* - Pr

9. A chocolate museum in St. Stephen houses the original Ganong factory. The Ganongs are Canada's oldest family-owned candy maker and the first <u>to introduce</u> the five cent chocolate bar. *(That must have been quite a few years ago!)*

Verbs: *houses* – Pr   *are* – Pr

10. Actor and movie star, Donald Sutherland, father of the television series "24" star, Keifer Sutherland, was introduced to the theatre through puppet classes at the New Brunswick museum in Saint John.

Verbs: *was introduced* – Pa

Nova Scotia

PRACTICE with VERBS – requiring a bit more thought

Verbs are action words that make our sentences interesting. As in any language, it does take some memorizing to use the tense of verbs correctly. Some simple examples are below. For more complete information about verbs go here:

perfect-english-grammar.com/verb-tenses.html

To speak about an action in the <u>present time</u>**, you would use the** *present tense* **of a verb.**

I <u>see</u> you are reading archive copies of the Halifax Gazette.

Do you <u>know</u> it is Canada's first newspaper printed in 1752?

We like <u>to swim</u> at Silver Sands beach because it <u>is</u> right on the ocean.

To speak about an action that occurred in the past, you would use the *past tense* **of a verb.**

I <u>saw</u> you touring St. Mary's University in Halifax.

You <u>learned</u> that Dalhousie University is famous for its medical faculty.

I <u>did not want</u> to visit Peggy's Cove today, I wanted to see the Maritime Museum.

To speak about an action that will happen in the future, you would use the *future tense.*

I <u>will meet</u> you at Tim Horton's in Halifax Shopping Centre tomorrow at noon.

We <u>will have </u>lobster rolls for lunch and then <u>we'll tour</u> the Citadel.

To speak about an action that might happen – but you're not sure it will – you would use the *conditional tense.*

We <u>could go</u> whale watching or we <u>might go</u> kayaking on the Bay of Fundy.

Maybe Sue <u>might not like</u> to go sailing on Banook Lake. Do you know if she swims?

Now it's your turn to list all the verbs and label them with the correct tense. Remember to include the infinitive form – the verbs with "to" in front of them.

Put a Pr if the verb is in the present tense; a Pa if it's in the past tense, an F if it's in the future tense, a C if it's in the conditional tense and an I if it is in the Infinitive form.

1. When I spent summers in Dartmouth, it was fun to take the small ferry across the water to Halifax. In 1955, the Angus L. MacDonald Bridge was built for a quick drive across the water. *(Then the fun was throwing the toll coins out the car window and hoping they would land in the basket!)*

2. Point Pleasant Park is a beautiful green-forested space at the south end of Halifax. In 1993 Hurricane Juan devastated its picturesque trails and downed hundreds of trees. It is slowly regaining its former beauty. *(It made me so sad when I saw this devastation.)*

3. One day, standing in Point Pleasant Park, I watched a tiny dot out in the Atlantic Ocean. As the dot grew larger, I could see it was a ship coming up over the *curve* of the ocean. *(I thought "Wow! I think I just saw that the earth really is round!" My dad said I had a vivid imagination.)*

4. One of the beaches where we used to swim was called Silver Sands. It was part of the Atlantic Ocean and it was *so* cold we felt every grain of sand in the salt water as it slid over us!

5. Tourism Nova Scotia says you can see whales off the coast but I never spotted any when I lived there. *(But I've sure seen them in British Columbia waters!)*

6. I remember driving through the Annapolis Valley in the fall and stopping to buy many varieties of apples. Just writing about them makes my mouth water!

7. Port Morien, Nova Scotia, claims that it was the home of the first Boy Scout troop in North America. The troop was founded in 1908, shortly after Robert Baden-Powell published the book *Scouting for Boys,* which inspired boys all over the word to form Scout troops.

8. Nova Scotia has more historic sites than any other province except Québec. That's amazing when you consider how small NS is compared to many other provinces. *(Probably this is because it's a much older province than those that are larger in size.)*

9. Alexander Graham Bell, a Scottish–Canadian, invented the telephone in 1877. Almost 140 years later, a major telephone company in North America still bears his name. He said the telephone was an "intrusion" on his real work and refused to have one in his study! He had many inventions, including things to help people who are deaf. *(Just Google his name to learn more.)*

10. Many tourists and scientists seek permission to visit Sable Island to see and study the protected feral horses. They resemble Spanish horses but are stocky with short legs that allow them to move easily on sandy or rough ground. *(Rick Mercer, one of Canada's best-loved comedians takes you on a tour of Sable Island on YouTube here: youtube.com/watch?v=kAldKJAgLo4)*

Answers on next page

In the following sentences, the verbs have been listed and labeled with the proper tense.

1. When I spent summers in Dartmouth, it was fun to take the small ferry across the water to Halifax. In 1955, the Angus L. MacDonald Bridge was built for a quick drive across the water. *(Then the fun was throwing the toll coins out the car window and hoping they would land in the basket!)*

Verbs: *spent* – Pa   *was* – Pa   *to take* – I   *was built* - Pa

2. Point Pleasant Park is a beautiful green-forested space at the south end of Halifax. In 1993 Hurricane Juan devastated its picturesque trails and downed hundreds of trees. It is slowly regaining its former beauty. *(It made me so sad when I saw this devastation.)*

Verbs: *is* – Pr   *devastated* – Pa   *downed* – Pa   *is* – Pr   *regaining* - Pr

3. One day, standing in Point Pleasant Park, I watched a tiny dot out in the Atlantic Ocean. As the dot grew larger, I could see it was a ship coming up over the *curve* of the ocean. *(I thought "Wow! I think I just saw that the earth really is round! My dad said I had a vivid imagination.")*

Verbs: *standing* – Pr   *watched* – Pa   *grew* – Pa   *could see* – C
was – Pa   *coming* - Pr

4. One of the beaches where we used to swim was called Silver Sands. It was part of the Atlantic Ocean and it was *so* cold we were sure we could feel *every* grain of sand in the salt water as it slid over us!

Verbs: *used* – Pa   *to swim* – I   *was called* – Pa   *was* – Pa   *was* – Pa
were sure – Pa   *could feel* – C   *slid* - Pa

5. Tourism Nova Scotia says you can see whales off the coast but I never spotted any when I lived there. *(But I've sure seen them in British Columbia waters!)*

Verbs: *says* – Pr   *can see* – Pr   *spotted* – Pa   *lived* - Pa

6. I remember driving through the Annapolis Valley in the fall and stopping to buy many varieties of apples. Just writing about them makes my mouth water!

Verbs: *remember* – Pr   *driving* – Pr   *stopping* – Pr   *to buy* – I
writing – Pr   *makes* - Pr

7. Port Morien, Nova Scotia, claims that it was the home of the first Boy Scout troop in North America. The troop was founded in 1908, shortly after Robert Baden-Powell published the book *Scouting for Boys,* which inspired boys all over the word to form Scout troops.

Verbs: *claims* – Pr   *was* – Pa   *was founded* – Pa   *published* – Pa
inspired – Pa   *to form* - I

8. Nova Scotia has more historic sites than any other province except Québec. That is amazing when you consider how small NS is compared to many other provinces. *(Maybe it's because it's one of Canada's oldest provinces, even though others are larger in size?)*

Verbs: *has* – Pr   *is* – Pr   *consider* – Pr   *is* - Pr

9. Alexander Graham Bell invented the telephone in 1877. Almost 140 years later, a major telephone company in North America still bears his name. He said the telephone was an "intrusion" on his real work and refused to have one in his study! He had many inventions, including things to help people who are deaf. *(Just Google his name to learn more.)*

Verbs: *invented* – Pa   *bears* – Pr   *had* – Pa   *said* – Pa   *was* – Pa
refused – Pa   *had* – Pa   *to help* – I   *are* – Pr

10. Many tourists and scientists seek permission to visit Sable Island to see and study the protected feral horses. They resemble Spanish horses but are stocky with short legs that allow them to move easily on sandy or rough ground.

Verbs: *seek*- Pr   *to visit* – I   *to see* – I *study* – Pr   *resemble* – Pr
are – Pr   *allow* - Pr   *to move* - I

Prince Edward Island

PRACTICE with VERBS - the more challenging ones!

Verbs are action words that make our sentences interesting. As in any language, it does take some memorizing to use the tense of verbs correctly, so let's use some simple examples here – for a good review. For more complete information about verbs go here:

perfect-english-grammar.com/verb-tenses.html

To speak about an action in the <u>present time</u>, you would use the *present tense* of a verb.
I <u>see</u> you are reading the book Anne of Green Gables by L.M. Montgomery. Do you <u>know</u> the University of Prince Edward Island is in Charlottetown? We like <u>to cross</u> the new bridge and <u>enjoy</u> a lobster roll in Shediac, NB!

To speak about an action that occurred in the past, you would use the *past tense* of a verb.
I <u>saw</u> you studying the map while planning your hike on the Sentier Trail. You <u>learned</u> that Singing Sands Beach is a very special one on the island. I <u>did not want</u> to visit PEI National Park this week I <u>preferred</u> to go to Cavendish.

To speak about an action that will happen in the future, you would use the *future tense.*
I <u>will meet</u> you at the Anne of Green Gables museum tomorrow afternoon. We <u>will enjoy</u> clams for lunch from the tearoom and <u>we'll sit</u> outdoors to eat.

To speak about an action that might happen – but you're not sure it will – you would use the *conditional tense.*
We <u>could try</u> an oyster stew at Tim Horton's or we <u>might play</u> tennis instead. She <u>might not like</u> hiking along the 273 km Confederation Trail.

Now it's your turn to find and list the verbs in the following sentences.
Put a *Pr* if the verb is in the present tense; a *Pa* if it's in the past tense,
an *F* if it's in the future tense and a *C* if it's in the conditional tense.

1. The 273 kilometers Federation Trail is open for you to walk, to cycle, to run or to go over by wheelchair in the summer. In the winter, you could cover it by snowshoe or snowmobile. You would go from one tip of the island to the other on old railway beds. *(No worries – trains don't travel there anymore.)*

2. For eight months of the year, a ferry will take you from Prince Edward Island to Caribou, Nova Scotia. In the summer, you could also take a five-hour ferry ride from Souris, PEI to the Magdalene Islands, which are part of the province of Québec.

3. The Confederation Bridge, completed in 1997, is the longest bridge in the world that goes over water that is covered with ice in winter.

4. Prince Edward island is famous for its beaches. With over 800 kilometers of beaches, it's hard to pick just one top beach, but the Internet site vacay.ca has decided. It names Singing Sands Beach in Basin Head Provincial Park the number one beach in Canada. *(High praise indeed for this tiny island!)*

5. The coastline provides great kayaking and you might like to take long walks between leisurely paddles to see many species of birds in the marsh grasses.

6. Paddling in a western bay, you will find warm water and shelter because of the protective effect of the barrier sand dunes. In places, they extend over 15 m high! *(Sounds like a good place to go sand boogy-boarding!)*

7. Malpeque Bay is famous for some of the world's most delicious oysters. On nearby islands in the spring, you might see eagles preparing to attack the cormorant nests.

8. The most snow ever to fall in PEI in one day is 48 cm. You would have seen many people shoveling on that day back on February 7, 1956. The

most snow to fall in a winter season was over 24 meters and occurred in 2014.

9. Lucy Maude Montgomery, a native of PEI, wrote the book *Anne of Green Gables,* which was published in 1908. It is set in the province near Cavendish Beach. You can visit the house that inspired the book. *(It's a National Historic Site now.)*

10. Prince Edward Island is on the Atlantic Time Zone – that's one more hour added to the Eastern Time Zone. Just to confuse time changes a little more, Newfoundland adds only 30 minutes to the Atlantic Time Zone. *("Newfoundlanders" love to be distinctive! But hey, they keep us on our toes, eh?)*

For extra practice, see if you can find 10 infinitive verb forms in the above sentences. They are the verbs with 'to' in front of them.

Answers on next page

In the following sentences, the verbs have been underlined and the tense noted under each sentence.

1. The 273-kilometer Federation Trail <u>is open</u> for you <u>to walk</u>, <u>to cycle</u>, <u>to run</u> or <u>to go</u> over by wheelchair in the summer. In the winter, you <u>could cover</u> it by snowshoe or snowmobile. You <u>would go</u> from one tip of the island to the other on old railway beds. *(No worries – trains don't travel there anymore.)*

Verbs: *is open* – Pr   *to walk* – I   *to cycle* – I   *to run* – I   *to go* - I
could cover – C   *would go* - C

2. For eight months of the year, a ferry <u>will take</u> you from Prince Edward Island to Caribou, Nova Scotia. In the summer, you <u>could also take</u> a five-hour ferry ride from Souris, PEI to the Magdalene Islands, which <u>are</u> part of the province of Québec.

Verbs: *will take* – F   *could also take* - C   *are* - Pr

3. The Confederation Bridge, <u>completed</u> in 1997, <u>is</u> the longest bridge in the world that <u>goes</u> over water that <u>is covered</u> with ice in winter.

Verbs: *completed* – Pa   *is* – Pr   *goes* - Pr   *is covered* - Pr

4. Prince Edward Island <u>is</u> famous for its beaches. With over 800 kilometers of beaches, it <u>is hard</u> <u>to pick</u> just one top beach, but the Internet site vacay.ca <u>has decided</u>. It <u>names</u> Singing Sands Beach in Basin Head Provincial Park the number one beach in Canada. *(High praise indeed!)*

Verbs: *is* - Pr   *is hard* – Pr   *to pick* – I   *has decided* – Pr   *names* - Pr

5. The coastline <u>provides</u> great kayaking and you <u>might like</u> <u>to take</u> long walks between wonderful paddles <u>to see</u> many species of birds in the marsh grasses.

Verbs: *provides* – Pr   *might like* – C   *to take* – I   *to see* - I

6. <u>Paddling</u> in a western bay, you <u>will find</u> warm water and shelter because of the protective effect of the barrier sand dunes. In places, they <u>extend</u> over 50 feet high! *(Sounds like a good place to go sand boogy-boarding!)*

Verbs: *paddling* – Pr   *will find* – F   *extend* - Pr

7. Malpeque Bay <u>is</u> famous for some of the world's most delicious oysters. On nearby islands in the spring, you <u>might see</u> eagles <u>preparing</u> <u>to attack</u> the cormorant nests.

Verbs: *is* – Pr   *might see* - C   *preparing* – Pr   *to attack* - I

8. The most snow ever <u>to fall</u> in PEI in one day <u>is</u> 48 cm. You <u>would have seen</u> many people <u>shoveling</u> on that day back on February 7, 1956. The most snow <u>to fall</u> in a winter season <u>was</u> over 24 meters and <u>occurred</u> in 2014.

Verbs: *to fall* – I   *is* – Pr   *would have seen* – C   *shoveling* – <u>Pr</u>
to fall – I   *was* - Pa   *occurred* - Pa

9. Lucy Maude Montgomery, a native of PEI, <u>wrote</u> the book *Anne of Green Gables,* which <u>was</u> <u>published</u> in 1908. It <u>is set</u> in the province near Cavendish Beach. You <u>can visit</u> the house that <u>inspired</u> the book. *(It's a National Historic Site now.)*

Verbs: *wrote* – Pa   *was published* – Pa   *is set* – Pr   *can visit* – Pr
inspired - Pa

10. Prince Edward Island <u>is</u> on the Atlantic Time Zone – that <u>is</u> one more hour <u>added</u> to the Eastern Time Zone. Just <u>to confuse</u> time changes a little more, Newfoundland <u>adds</u> only 30 minutes to the Atlantic Time Zone. *("Newfoundlanders" love to be distinctive! But, hey, they keep us on our toes, eh?)*

Verbs: *is* – Pr   *is* - Pr   *added* – Pr   *to confuse* – I   *adds* - Pr

For extra practice – the Infinitive form of the verb has been labeled with an I.

Quebec

PRACTICE with ADJECTIVES – some very colourful ones!

An <u>adjective</u> is a descriptive word. We wouldn't have very colourful language if we didn't use many of these in our conversation! We use adjectives to give more information about nouns – names of persons, places or things or pronouns – that can take the place of nouns.

Note the underlined adjectives in these examples.

> About <u>22 million</u> tourists visit Québec each year to see its <u>historical</u> landmarks and to experience its <u>breathtaking</u> scenery.

> Montréal offers tourists <u>historic</u> attractions, and <u>beautiful</u> parks. One of them on the <u>green</u> slopes of Mount Royal, provides an <u>idyllic</u> place to rest after a <u>marathon</u> <u>shopping</u> spree.

Now it's your turn to find and underline all the adjectives in the following sentences.

1. The early construction of the beautiful St. Joseph's Oratory in Montréal began in 1904. It was enlarged twice and was finally completed in 1967. It is the largest church in Canada and its magnificent dome is the third largest in the world.

2. The prestigious McGill University in Montréal, founded in 1821, is Canada's most international university. Its graduates include 10 Nobel Prize Winners - the highest among all other Canadian universities. *(All Canadian universities are public institutions and there are 90 presently in Canada. Quest, in Squamish, British Columbia, is Canada's first independent, not-for-profit, secular university. It opened in 2007 and offers only one degree, a Bachelor of Arts and Sciences.)*

3. The Québec Citadel is a functioning military installation for Canada's Armed Forces. It also houses an official residence for the Governor General of Canada, the Queen's representative in this country. The Governor General's other imposing residence is Rideau Hall, 1 Sussex Drive, Ottawa, Ontario.

**La Citadelle de Québec is next to the Plains
of Abraham on the St. Lawrence River**

4. This star-shaped fortress was built in the late 1800s and has 25 amazingly maintained buildings for tourists to see. It also contains an interesting military museum. *(Historic notes are in both French and English. That's good for me because I have forgotten so many French words ☹ C'est terrible!)*

3. In June 1896, Louis Minier and Louis Pupier presented a movie at the exciting Palace Theatre in Montréal. This was the first movie *ever* shown in North America. *(I didn't know that! Incroyable!)*

6. Two Montréal journalists invented the incredibly popular general knowledge game *Trivial Pursuit*. They had wanted to play Scrabble but some key tiles were missing, so they created their own game and marketed this well-liked game in 1982. Millions of the fascinating games were sold in almost 20 countries. In 2008, the well-known Hasbro toys and puzzles company, bought the rights to this genius game for $80 million US. *(Not bad for pursuing an idea that saved them from being bored!)*

7. In the New Brunswick Chapter, you have read about the well-publicized Magnetic Hill just outside Moncton, New Brunswick. There is also a Côte Magnétique just outside Chartierville, Québec that is not "marketed" as

strongly to attract thousands of tourists. However, it still "works." There is just a small sign that reads: "Stop here. Put car in neutral. Look behind and experiment. Have a nice day!" ☺ *(Gotta love the simplicity, oui?)*

8. Lake Memphremagog lies between the USA State of Vermont and the Canadian Province of Québec. Apparently, the lake has an elusive " monster" called "Memphre." It has received sightings since the 19th century and continues on in the folklore of the area. *(Doesn't this sound vaguely familiar? Think – Scotland – Loch Ness!)*

9. North America's only **Ice Hotel**, located just west of Québec City, is open from January to April. It's made of about 360 tonnes of ice and 11,000 tonnes of snow and has 34 frigid rooms. *(Better take an extra warm sleeping bag especially if you just want to sit in the icy bar for an ice cold drink!)*

10. Marc Garneau from Québec City was the first Canadian astronaut to enter space. He flew on the splendid space shuttle *Challenger* in 1984 and on the enormous *Endeavour* in 1996 and 2000. He is one of 12 Canadians who have been selected to become astronauts. Did you notice E*ndeavour* is spelled the British/Canadian way and not the American way *(Endeavor)*? If you are curious to find out why, just go on the Internet to: space_shuttle_endeavour *(I think the reason is really special!)*

Answers on next page

In the following sentences, all the adjectives have been underlined.

1. The <u>early</u> construction of the <u>beautiful</u> St. Joseph's Oratory in Montréal began in 1904. It was enlarged twice and was finally completed in 1967. It is the <u>largest</u> church in Canada and its <u>magnificent</u> dome is the <u>third largest</u> in the world.

2. The <u>prestigious</u> McGill University in Montréal, founded in 1821, is Canada's most <u>international</u> university. Its graduates include 10 <u>Nobel Prize</u> Winners - the highest among all <u>other Canadian</u> universities. *(All Canadian universities are public institutions and there are 90 presently in Canada. Quest, in Squamish, British Columbia, is the first non-profit independent university in Canada. It opened in 2007.)*

3. The Québec Citadel is a functioning <u>military</u> installation for Canada's Armed Forces. It also houses an <u>official</u> residence for the Governor General of Canada, the <u>Queen's</u> representative in this country. The Governor General's other <u>imposing</u> residence is Rideau Hall, 1 Sussex Drive, Ottawa, Ontario.

4. This <u>star-shaped</u> fortress was built in the <u>late</u> 1800s and has <u>25</u> amazingly <u>maintained</u> buildings for tourists to see. It also contains an <u>interesting military</u> museum. *(Historic notes are in both French and English. That's good for me because I have forgotten so many French words ☹ C'est terrible!)*

5. In June 1896, Louis Minier and Louis Pupier presented a movie at the <u>exciting</u> Palace Theatre in Montréal. This was the <u>first</u> movie *ever* shown in North America. *(I didn't know that! Incroyable!)*

6. <u>Two</u> <u>Montréal</u> journalists invented the incredibly <u>popular</u> <u>general knowledge</u> game *Trivial Pursuit*. They had wanted to play Scrabble but some <u>key</u> tiles were missing so they created their <u>own</u> game and marketed this <u>well-liked</u> game in 1982. Millions of the <u>fascinating</u> games were sold in almost <u>20</u> countries. In 2008, the <u>well-known</u> Hasbro toys and puzzles company bought the rights to this <u>genius</u> game for $80 million US. *(Not bad for pursuing an idea that saved them from being bored!)*

7. In the New Brunswick Chapter, you have read about the <u>well-publicized</u> Magnetic Hill just outside Moncton, New Brunswick. There is also a Côte

Magnétique just outside Chartierville, Québec that is not "marketed" as strongly to attract <u>thousands</u> of tourists. However, it still "works." There is just a <u>small</u> sign that reads: "Stop here. Put car in neutral. Look behind and experiment. Have a <u>nice</u> day!" ☺ *(Gotta love the simplicity, oui?)*

8. Lake Memphremagog lies between the <u>USA</u> State of Vermont and the <u>Canadian</u> Province of Québec. Apparently, the lake has an <u>elusive</u> "monster" called "Memphre." It has received <u>several</u> sightings since the <u>18th</u> century and continues on in the folklore of the area. *(Doesn't this sound vaguely familiar? Think – Scotland – Loch Ness?)*

9. North America's only <u>Ice</u> **Hotel**, located just west of Québec City, is open from January to April. It's made of about <u>360</u> tonnes of ice and <u>11,000</u> tonnes of snow and has <u>34</u> <u>frigid</u> rooms. *(Better take an extra warm sleeping bag especially if you just want to sit in the "Ice Bar" for an ice cold drink!)*

10. Marc Garneau from Québec City, was the <u>first</u> <u>Canadian</u> astronaut to enter space. He flew on the <u>splendid</u> <u>space</u> shuttle *Challenger* in 1984 and on the <u>enormous</u> *Endeavour* in 1996 and 2000. He is one of <u>12</u> Canadians who have been selected to become astronauts. Did you notice E*ndeavour* is spelled the British/Canadian way and not the American way *(Endeavor)*? If you are curious to find out why, *(I think the reason is really special!)* just go on the Internet here:

space_shuttle_endeavour

Ontario

PRACTICE with ADJECTIVES - just a few more!

An <u>adjective</u> is a descriptive word. We wouldn't have very colourful language if we didn't use many of these in our conversation! We use adjectives to give more information about nouns – names of persons, places or things.

Note the underlined adjectives in these examples.

In the <u>early</u> spring, Ottawa is ablaze with colour from <u>thousands</u> of <u>beautiful</u> tulips.

In 1945, the <u>Dutch Royal</u> family sent <u>100,000</u> <u>tulip</u> bulbs to Ottawa in gratitude for Canadians having sheltered Princess Juliana and her daughters for the <u>preceding</u> <u>three</u> years during World War II.

The <u>grateful</u> Netherlands continues to send <u>thousands</u> of bulbs to Canada <u>each</u> year, and the <u>annual</u> Tulip Festival now features nearly <u>three million</u> bulbs planted around Ottawa.

Now it's your turn to underline all the adjectives in the following sentences.

1. The old stone Parliament buildings in busy downtown Ottawa have their own unique appeal.

2. There is great rivalry between the popular Ottawa Senators hockey team and the newest Canadian team in Manitoba called the Winnipeg Jets.

3. Basketball is not a very popular sport in Canada compared to the USA, even though a Canadian, Dr. James Naismith, invented the exciting game in 1891!

4. Ice skating on the frozen Rideau Canal is a well-liked pastime in Ottawa during the very cold winter days.

5. When you visit Canada's capital city, Ottawa, in spring, try to be there for the Tulip Festival. You will see the millions of beautiful tulips sent each year by a grateful Dutch Royal Family.

6. Most Canadians usually think of the "centre" of Canada to be somewhere in Québec or Ontario, since we call these provinces "Central 'Canada'.' Actually, there are several ways to determine Canada's "centre" each way giving a different spot. One way, determines it's a little west of Winnipeg. *(I think that's the one I'll try to remember!)*

7. Stephen Leacock, one of Canada's most beloved humourists, wrote the entertaining book *Sunshine Sketches of a Little Town.* It was first published in 1912 and has remained popular due to its universal appeal. A TV movie was adapted from the light-hearted book in 2012 to celebrate the book's one-hundredth anniversary of its first publication.

8. The first person to go over Niagara Falls in a wooden barrel and survive was Annie Edson Taylor in 1901. She was a 62 year-old schoolteacher who had lost her job and who thought this stunt would gain her "fame and fortune." Unfortunately, her feat was not a big moneymaker! *(She should have been called "Lucky Annie" after surviving the falls!)*

9. More yummy fruits and delicious vegetables are produced in Ontario than in any other province or territory in Canada. Ontario has a good growing season in rich soil near Lake Ontario. The Niagara Peninsula is the site of the largest wine-producing region in Canada. Wines in this region range from traditional grape varieties and fruit wines to the cool-climate varieties as well. *(I guess British Columbia must be a close second with its large Okanagan wine region.)*

10. Hamilton resident, George Klein, created the first electric wheelchair in 1952. He also helped develop the first nuclear reactor outside the USA. He also created the gearing system on the Canadarm, the remote-controlled mechanical arm used to capture and repair satellites. *(Mr. Klein seems to have been "on a roll" with inventions!)*

Answers on next page

All the adjectives have been underlined in the following sentences.

1. The <u>old</u> <u>stone</u> Parliament buildings in <u>busy</u> <u>downtown</u> Ottawa have their <u>own</u> <u>unique</u> appeal.

2. There is <u>great</u> rivalry between the <u>popular</u> Ottawa Senators <u>hockey</u> team and the <u>newest</u> <u>Canadian</u> team in Manitoba called the Winnipeg Jets.

3. Basketball is not a very <u>popular</u> sport in Canada compared to the USA, even though a Canadian, Dr. James Naismith, invented the <u>exciting</u> game in 1891!

4. <u>Ice</u> skating on the <u>frozen</u> Rideau Canal is a <u>well-liked</u> pastime in Ottawa during the very <u>cold</u> <u>winter</u> days.

5. When you visit Canada's <u>capital</u> city, Ottawa, in spring, try to be there for the <u>Tulip</u> Festival. You will see the <u>millions</u> of <u>beautiful</u> tulips sent <u>each</u> year by a <u>grateful</u> <u>Royal</u> Family.

6. <u>Most</u> Canadians usually think of the "centre" of Canada to be somewhere in Québec or Ontario, since we call <u>these</u> provinces "Central 'Canada".' Actually, there are <u>several</u> ways to determine Canada's "centre," <u>each</u> way giving a <u>different</u> spot. <u>One</u> way, determines it's a <u>little</u> west of Winnipeg. *(I think that's the one I'll try to remember!)*

7. Stephen Leacock, one of Canada's most <u>beloved</u> humourists, wrote the <u>entertaining</u> book *Sunshine Sketches of a Little Town.* It was first published in 1912 and has remained popular due to its <u>universal</u> appeal. A <u>TV</u> movie was adapted from the <u>light-hearted</u> book in 2012 to celebrate the book's <u>one-hundredth</u> anniversary of its <u>first</u> publication.

8. The <u>first</u> person to go over Niagara Falls in a <u>wooden</u> barrel and survive was Annie Edson Taylor in 1901. She was a <u>62 year-old</u> schoolteacher who had lost her job and who thought <u>this</u> stunt would gain her "fame and fortune." Unfortunately, her feat was not a <u>big</u> <u>moneymaker</u>! *(She should have been called "Lucky Annie" after surviving the falls!)*

9. <u>More</u> <u>yummy</u> fruits and <u>delicious</u> vegetables are produced in Ontario than in <u>any</u> <u>other</u> province or territory in Canada. Ontario has a <u>good</u> <u>growing</u> season in <u>rich</u> soil near Lake Ontario. The Niagara Peninsula

is the site of the largest <u>wine-producing</u> region in Canada. Wines in this region range from <u>traditional</u> grape varieties and <u>fruit</u> wines to the <u>cool-climate</u> varieties as well. *(I think British Columbia must be a close second with its large Okanagan wine region.)*

10. <u>Hamilton</u> resident, George Klein, created the first <u>electric</u> wheelchair in 1952. He also helped develop the first <u>nuclear</u> reactor outside the USA. He also created the <u>gearing</u> system on the Canadarm, the <u>remote-controlled</u> <u>mechanical</u> arm used to capture and repair satellites. *(Mr. Klein seems to have been "on a roll" with inventions!)*

Manitoba

PRACTICE with ADVERBS

An **adverb** can modify (explain more about) a verb, an adjective, another adverb, a phrase or a clause. An adverb indicates manner, time, place, cause, or degree and answers questions such as "how," "when," "where," and "how much".

Some adverbs can be identified by their "ly" suffix. Most of them, however, can be identified by how they work in a sentence or clause as a whole. Unlike an adjective, an adverb can be found in various places within the sentence.

> You may find more information on adverbs on the Internet here: grammar.ccc.commnet.edu/grammar/adverbs.htm

Examples:

D'Arcy McGee, was a federal politician who was a loyal supporter of Confederation. Unfortunately, in April 1868, he was killed in Ottawa a week before his forty-third birthday. He had almost entered his house when he was shot. His assassin, Patrick J. Whelan, was subsequently hanged later that year.

Over a period of many years, Nellie McClung patiently advocated for women's financial independence.

Now it's your turn to find and underline the adverbs in the following sentences.

1. Churchill, Manitoba, is commonly referred to as the "Polar Bear Capital."

2. Immigrants from the Highlands of Scotland primarily managed The North West Company.

3. Travelling across Manitoba, you would soon see not only fields of yellow Canola plants but also in the north, the huge nickel mines.

4. Tommy Douglas is considered to be "The Greatest Canadian," because we owe our Medicare System to his relentless pursuit of affordable healthcare for all Canadians.

5. Since 1976, all of Canada's coins – loonies, toonies, quarters, dimes, and nickels - have been loyally produced in the Royal Canadian Mint in southeastern Winnipeg.

6. Carol Shields wrote most of her books while always living in Winnipeg. She was amazingly brilliant to have *The Stone Diaries* be the only book to ever receive both the 1995 Pulitzer Prize for Fiction and the 1993 Governor General's Award.

7. It is not very often that a town in Canada is named after a science fiction character. Flin Flon is named after Professor Josiah Flintabbatey Flonatin. He was a fictitious character, in a 1905 paperback adventure novel *The Sunless City* by J.E. Muddock. A prospector, Thomas Creighton, was quickly reminded of the book when he discovered a rich vein of copper by a deep lake. He called it Flin Flon's mine, thankfully shortening the name!

8. Parts of Manitoba have genuinely scary Hallowe'en nights and one of the scariest is in Churchill. In this "Polar Bear Capital of the World," parents specifically warn kids not to wear furry white costumes. They are also to immediately take cover if they hear the sound of "fire crackers" (a.k.a. gunshots). That's because this is the time of year polar bears are persistently hunting day and night in anticipation of winter.

9. How about taking a leisurely visit to the Assiniboine Park's 1100 acres in Winnipeg? You could quickly take pictures of 8000 flowers, plants and trees in the botanical garden. Later, you could slowly refresh yourself by listening to a band in the park's Lyric Theatre.

10. At the Lower Fort Garry National Historic Site, you might be pleasantly surprised by "early settlers" (students and volunteers in period costumes) excitedly explaining what life was like back in the 1700s. This is the oldest intact stone fort in western Canada. It was built in 1812 and it passionately preserves much of the atmosphere of the Red River colony.

Answers on next page

All the adverbs have been underlined in the following sentences.

1. Churchill, Manitoba, is <u>commonly</u> referred to as the "Polar Bear Capital."

2. Immigrants from the Highlands of Scotland, <u>primarily</u> managed The North West Company.

3. Travelling across Manitoba, you would <u>soon</u> see not only fields of yellow Canola plants but also in the north, the huge nickel mines.

4. Tommy Douglas is considered to be "The Greatest Canadian," because we owe our Medicare System to his <u>relentless</u> pursuit of affordable healthcare for all Canadians.

5. Since 1976, all of Canada's coins – loonies, toonies, quarters, dimes, and nickels - have been <u>loyally</u> produced in the Royal Canadian Mint in southeastern Winnipeg.

6. Carol Shields wrote most of her books while <u>always</u> living in Winnipeg. She was amazingly brilliant to have *The Stone Diaries* be the only book to <u>ever</u> receive both the 1993 Governor General's Award, and the 1995 Pulitzer Prize for Fiction.

7. It is not <u>very</u> often that a town in Canada is named after a science fiction character. Flin Flon is named after Professor Josiah Flintabbatey Flonatin. He was a fictitious character in a 1905 paperback adventure novel *The Sunless City* by J. E. Muddock. A prospector, Thomas Creighton, was <u>quickly</u> reminded of the book when he discovered a rich vein of copper by a deep lake. He called it Flin Flon's mine, <u>thankfully</u> shortening the name!

8. Parts of Manitoba have genuinely scary Hallowe'en nights and one of the scariest is in Churchill. In this "Polar Bear Capital of the World," parents <u>specifically</u> warn kids not to wear furry white costumes. They are also to <u>immediately</u> take cover if they hear the sound of "fire crackers" (a.k.a. gunshots). That's because this is the time of year polar bears are <u>persistently</u> hunting day and night in anticipation of winter.

9. How about taking a leisurely visit to the Assiniboine Park's 1100 acres in Winnipeg? You could quickly take pictures of 8000 flowers, plants and trees in the botanical garden. Later, you could slowly refresh yourself by listening to a band in the park's Lyric Theatre.

10. At the Lower Fort Garry National Historic Site, you might be pleasantly surprised by "early settlers" (students and volunteers in period costumes) excitedly explaining what life was like back in the 1700s. This is the oldest intact stone fort in western Canada. It was built in 1812 and it passionately preserves much of the atmosphere of the Red River colony.

Saskachewan

PRACTICE with ADVERBS – a chance to choose your own!

An adverb is added to a verb to modify its meaning. Usually, an adverb tells when, where, how, in what manner, or to what extent, an action is performed. Many adverbs end in ly – especially ones that are used to express how an action is performed. Adverbs may also give more information about an adjective or another adverb.

More information on adverbs may be found in these (and many more!) Internet sites:
grammar-monster.com/lessons/adverbs.htm
grammar.com/adverb/

> *Examples:*
> *The little polar bear ran the <u>fastest</u> he had ever run from the wolf pack.*
> *The singer sang <u>softly</u> so as not to disturb the sleeping children.*

Now it's your turn to choose the adverb you think fits the best in the following sentences. You may have to choose more than one in each sentence. Whichever adverb you choose will be correct.

For <u>extra practice</u> you could note whether the adverb you have chosen tells when, where, how, in what manner, or to what extent and action is performed.

1. Saskatchewan is *(very, simply)* famous for its wonderful community spirit.

2. Edouard Beaupré was born in Willow Bunch, Saskatchewan, the eldest of 20 children, and at age 9 years, he *(quickly, suddenly)* became the tallest, reaching 6 feet (1.83 m). He grew at an *(alarming, amazing)* rate and by age 20 he was over 8 feet 9.9 inches (2.69 m) tall and weighed 400 lbs. (180 kg). He decided *(ultimately, finally)* to use his size to support his family. *(I left measurements in both systems so you could quickly see how extremely large this man was without having to do your own conversion!)*

3. Beaupré was called the "Willow Bunch Giant" and he toured the North American freak show circuit. He wrestled strong men and would *(often, willingly)* perform feats of strength.

4. Corner Gas is the *(most, least)* successful Canadian sitcom ever. It was set and filmed in Rouleau, Saskatchewan and ran for six seasons. There is now an official provincial holiday named Corner Gas Day, April 13th. *(I'm not sure what the special thing is that people do on that day!)*

5. The underground tunnels in Moose Jaw, built in the early 1900s, were to connect the heating systems of downtown buildings. They *(also, eventually)* became famous after being used by the notorious gangster, Al Capone's gang.

6. The town of Porcupine Plain, east of Saskatoon, welcomes visitors with "Quilly Willy," a statue of the world's largest porcupine. This mascot is 4 metres tall so hopefully he will not *(cheerfully, enthusiastically)* welcome you with a prickly hug!

7. If you like dancing, you might want to glide on down to Danceland in Watrous, Saskatchewan. When it was built in 1928, rolls of horsehair were *(carefully, meticulously)* wrapped in burlap and formed 2 subfloors under the maple hardwood floor. This allows the floor to 'give' up to 4 cm and dancers seem to *(easily, almost)* g l i d e across the floor.

8. Saskatchewan has always declined to follow the rest of Canada and change the clocks to have Daylight Saving Time. It says very *(strongly, adamantly)* that it has enough hours in the day.

9. Do you *(often, never)* wear a hoodie? A kangaroo? Or just a hooded sweatshirt? If it has a pocket in front to keep your hands warm, in Saskatchewan it's called a bunny hug. *(Cute!)*

10. No matter where you travel in Canada, you will probably see a Lee Valley Hardware store. The entrepreneur, who created this store that sells innovative gardening tools, was born in rural Saskatchewan. He grew up in a log cabin without electricity or running water. Perhaps this is what has made him *(eventually, amazingly)* an inventor.

Answers on next page

Answers for extra practice are included:

1. Saskatchewan is *(very - to what extent; simply – in what manner)* famous for its wonderful community spirit.

2. Edouard Beaupré was born in Willow Bunch, Saskatchewan, the eldest of 20 children, and at age 9 years, he *(quickly – in what manner; suddenly - how)* became the tallest, reaching 6 feet (1.83 m). He grew at an *(alarming – in what manner; amazing – in what manner)* rate and by age 20 he was over 8 feet 9.9 inches (2.69 m) tall and weighed 400 lbs. (180 kg). He decided *(ultimately – when; finally - when)* to use his size to support his family.

3. Beaupré was called the "Willow Bunch Giant" and he toured the North American freak show circuit. He wrestled strong men and would *(often – when; willingly – in what manner)* perform feats of strength.

4. Corner Gas is the *(most – to what extent; greatest – to what extent)* successful Canadian sitcom ever. It was set and filmed in Rouleau, Saskatchewan and ran for six seasons. There is now an official provincial holiday named Corner Gas Day, April 13th. *(I'm not sure what the special thing is that people do on that day.)*

5. The underground tunnels in Moose Jaw, built in the early 1900s, were to connect the heating systems of downtown buildings. They *(also – how; eventually - when)* became famous after being used by the notorious gangster, Al Capone's gang.

6. The town of Porcupine Plain, east of Saskatoon, welcomes visitors with "Quilly Willy," a statue of the world's largest porcupine. This mascot is 4 metres tall so hopefully he will not *(cheerfully – in what manner; enthusiastically – in what manner)* welcome you with a prickly hug!

7. If you like dancing, you might want to glide on down to Danceland in Watrous, Saskatchewan. When it was built in 1928, rolls of horsehair were *(carefully – how; meticulously - how)* wrapped in burlap and formed 2 subfloors under the maple hardwood floor. This allows the floor to 'give' up to 4 cm and dancers seem to almost g l i d e across the floor.

8. Saskatchewan has always declined to follow the rest of Canada and change the clocks to have Daylight Saving Time. It says very *(strongly – how; adamantly - how)* that it has enough hours in the day.

9. Do you *(often – when; never - when)* wear a hoodie? A kangaroo? Or just a hooded sweatshirt? If it has a pocket in front to keep your hands warm, in Saskatchewan it's called a bunny hug. *(Cute!)*

10. No matter where you travel in Canada, you will probably see a Lee Valley Hardware store. The entrepreneur who created this store that sells innovative gardening tools was born in rural Saskatchewan and grew up in a log cabin without electricity or running water. Perhaps this is what has made him *(eventually – when; amazingly - how)* an inventor.

Alberta

PRACTICE with ADVERBS – amazing ones!

An adverb usually tells when, where, how, in what manner, or to what extent, an action is performed. Many adverbs end in ly – especially ones that are used to express how an action is performed.

Other words that are adverbs include fast, never, well, very, most, least, more, less, now, far, and there. Adverbs may also give more information about an adjective or another adverb.

More information on adverbs may be found in these (and many more!) Internet sites:

grammar-monster.com/lessons/adverbs.htm
grammar.com/adverb/

There are thousands of adverbs, and each one can usually be categorized in one of the following groupings:

Adverbs of Time *(when)*	The black bear is approaching right *now*! We went fishing *daily* on the Peace River.
Adverbs of Place *(where)*	The wild rose grows almost *everywhere* in Alberta. *Somewhere* there are great ski hills in Alberta.
Adverbs of Manner *(how)*	With our binoculars we could easily see the mountain goats. We walked *steadily* around the Edmonton Mall for hours!
Adverbs of Degree *(extent)*	Fort McMurray is the *farthest* north I have ever travelled.

Now it's your turn to underline the adverbs in these sentences. There may be more than one in a sentence.

1. Many tourists visit the Village of Glendon to see the ridiculously oversized *pyrogy.

(*A delicious, filled dumpling (per-o-gi) that is loved by Ukrainians)

2. To see inside the world's largest dinosaur, you must cautiously climb the 106 stairs from its huge right leg, moving smoothly up into its cavernous mouth. From there you can quickly jump onto a 25 metre high viewing platform. *(I'll pass, thanks!)*

3. In the fur trading of the 1780s, what became widely know as The Hudson's Bay point wool blanket was greatly desired by Aboriginal tribes and traded for beaver pelts, buffalo robes, moccasins and other trade goods. *(I received one as a wedding present and it's truly heavy! The little black "points" tell how many pelts (historically) were traded for it.)*

4. Just for fun, you may want to check out St. Albert, the home of the world's largest badminton racquet, steadily standing just outside the Red Willow Badminton Club. You absolutely cannot miss seeing it, as it is an enormous 4.3 metres tall.

5. There is an extremely weird ghost in the Empress Theatre in Fort MacLeod. "Ed" is apparently the former resident janitor, and has been known to nonchalantly flip popcorn containers out of the trash when the theatre is always empty.

6. The Rocky Mountains were an enormous challenge to builders of the Canadian Pacific Railway. In some places craggy canyon walls had to be cautiously blasted out and workers would dangle dangerously over cliffs to fill blasting holes in the mountains.

7. Sometimes in the winter, warm winds called "Chinooks" silently stream across the Rockies bringing relief from the cold in Calgary and Edmonton.

8. The Columbia Icefield is a remnant of the great ice sheet that once covered most of Canada. Visitors enthusiastically take tours of the area in specially designed ice explorer vehicles.

9. Nickelback, a Canadian rock band from Hanna, Alberta, was formed in 1995. It is one of the most commercially successful Canadian groups, having sold over 35 million albums worldwide

10. Country music is very popular in Alberta. Ian Tyson (of Ian and Sylvia fame in the '60s), still lives there and k.d. lang was a popular singer in the '90s. Edmonton yearly hosts an International Jazz Festival and the symphony orchestras and opera companies of both Edmonton and Calgary regularly attract enthusiasts from all over North America.

Answers on next page

All the adverbs have been underlined in the following sentences.

1. Many tourists visit the Village of Glendon to see the <u>ridiculously</u> oversized *pyrogy.

    (*A delicious, filled dumpling (per-o-gi) that is loved by Ukrainians)

2. To see inside the world's largest dinosaur, you must <u>cautiously</u> climb the 106 stairs from its huge right leg, moving <u>smoothly</u> up into its cavernous mouth. From there you can <u>quickly</u> jump onto a 25 metre high viewing platform. *(I'll pass, thanks!)*

3. In the fur trading of the 1780s, what became <u>widely</u> know as The Hudson's Bay point wool blanket, was <u>greatly</u> desired by Aboriginal tribes and <u>often</u> traded for beaver pelts, buffalo robes, moccasins and other trade goods. *(I received one as a wedding present and it's truly heavy! The little black "points" tell how many pelts were traded for it.)*

4. Just for fun, you may want to check out St. Albert, the home of the world's largest badminton racquet, standing <u>steadily</u> just outside the Red Willow Badminton Club. You <u>absolutely</u> cannot miss seeing it, as it is an enormous 4.3 metres tall.

5. There is an <u>extremely</u> weird ghost in the Empress Theatre in Fort MacLeod. "Ed" is <u>apparently</u> the former resident janitor, and has been known to <u>nonchalantly</u> flip popcorn containers out of the trash when the theatre is <u>always</u> empty.

6. The Rocky Mountains were an enormous challenge to builders of the Canadian Pacific Railway. In some places, craggy canyon walls had to be <u>cautiously</u> blasted out and workers would dangle <u>dangerously</u> over cliffs to fill blasting holes in the mountains.

7. <u>Sometimes</u> in the winter, warm winds called "Chinooks" <u>silently</u> stream across the Rockies bringing relief from the cold in Calgary and Edmonton.

8. The Columbia Icefield is a remnant of the great ice sheet that <u>once</u> covered most of Canada. Visitors <u>enthusiastically</u> take tours of the area in <u>specially</u> designed ice explorer vehicles.

9. Nickelback, a Canadian rock band from Hanna, Alberta, was formed in 1995. It is one of the <u>most</u> commercially successful Canadian groups, having sold over 35 million albums <u>worldwide</u>.

10. Country music is <u>very</u> popular in Alberta. Ian Tyson (of Ian and Sylvia fame in the '60s), <u>still</u> lives there and k.d. lang was a popular singer in the '90s. Edmonton <u>yearly</u> hosts an International Jazz Festival. The symphony orchestras and opera companies of Edmonton and Calgary <u>regularly</u> attract enthusiasts from all over North America.

British Columbia

PRACTICE with PREPOSITIONS

There are about 150 prepositions in English. I'm sure you already know a lot of them – such as **from**, **in, of**, and **to**. They are among the most frequent words used in English.

Here are a few common examples*:*

*The larger cities **of** British Columbia are **in** the south of the province.*

*You must drive **from** Vancouver **through** the Interior before seeing the Rockies.*

*Be looking **for** the beautiful wildflowers **along** the roadways **in** British Columbia.*

*Walking **across** the suspension bridge **over** the Capilano River is much safer now than when it was first built **in** 1889 **of** just cedar planks strung together **with** hemp rope.*

Many of the more common one-word prepositions in this short list, have more than one meaning, so it's best to refer to a dictionary for the precise meaning and usage.

about above across after against along amid among around as at

before behind below beneath beside besides between beyond but by

concerning considering despite down during except excluding excepting

following for from in inside into like minus near of off on onto

opposite outside over past per plus regarding round save since than

through to toward towards under underneath unlike until up upon

versus via with within without

Now it's your turn to choose the preposition you think fits best in the following sentences:

1. Québec may be the province with the highest percentage of recreational cannabis smokers, (as, but) BC grows about 40% of the total Canadian crop of marijuana.

2. British Columbia has incredible waterfalls and Della Falls on Vancouver Island is the tallest one (about, in) Canada. (440 meters)

3. Totem poles have been (around, beyond) since the 1700s and they used to be small carvings. But (in, towards) the 19th century they became tree-sized carvings (of, near) colourful image (upon, within) image. The bigger a family's totem, the more status they had.

4. The Grey Cup, now the Canadian Football League's annual hard-fought trophy, was originally awarded (over, to) Canada's top amateur rugby team.

5. If you like watching amazing aerobatics (about, with) vintage planes, modern jets, and the Canadian Snowbirds team, come (toward, to) the Abbotsford Air Show the first weekend (around, in) August. It's a phenomenal annual event!

6. Russia sold Alaska (at, to) the United States (at, for) less than two cents an acre because Russia considered the British an enemy. That meant the Yukon had no access (beneath, to) the sea.

7. British Columbia Ferries operates 40 vessels and handles (beyond, about) 22 million passengers per year. They are especially busy in tourist season! *(Best to make a reservation!)*

8. The first international fair ever held (at, in) British Columbia was Expo 86. Some argued it was a waste (off, of) money that could be spent (on, into) education or health care. However, it brought a surge (for, of) tourist dollars and left Vancouver (with, via) a new transit system. The fair attracted participation (through, from) 41 countries and 22 million visitors saw Vancouver, many (within, for) the first time.

9. Skookumchuk Rapids (following, in) the Chinook Language means "turbulent water." This is just one (unlike, of) the many tourist attractions (around, in) British Columbia. *(Skookumchuk... what a fantastic name, eh?)*

10. A former copper mine (for, in) Britannia Beach is opened monthly (from, to) the public and is now a National Historic Site. *(Local school children received free tour tickets at the end of each school year. I went on the tour with our two children in about 1980. It made me much more aware of working conditions for miners. I remember that one machine they showed us over one mile underground (!) was called a "widow-maker." I also remember hoping the tour would end soon!)*

Answers on next page

Here are the prepositions that seem to fit best in the following sentences:

1. Québec may be the province with the highest percentage of recreational cannabis smokers, **but** BC grows about 40% of the total Canadian crop of marijuana.

2. British Columbia has incredible waterfalls and Della Falls on Vancouver Island is the tallest one **in** Canada (440 meters).

3. Totem poles have been **around** since the 1700s and they used to be small carvings. But **in** the 19th century, they became tree-sized carvings **of** colourful image **upon** image. The bigger a family's totem, the more status they had.

4. The Grey Cup, now the Canadian Football League's annual hard-fought trophy, was originally awarded **to** Canada's top amateur rugby team.

5. If you like watching amazing aerobatics **with** vintage planes, modern jets, and the Canadian Snowbirds team, come **to** the Abbotsford Air Show the first weekend **in** August. It's a phenomenal annual event!

6. Russia sold Alaska **to** the United States **for** less than two cents an acre because Russia considered the British an enemy. That left the Yukon with no access **to** the sea.

7. British Columbia Ferries operates 40 vessels and handles **about** 22 million passengers per year. They are especially busy in tourist season! *(It's best if you make a reservation!)*

8. The first international fair ever held **in** British Columbia was Expo 86. Some argued it was a waste **of** money that could be spent **on** education or health care. However, it brought a surge **of** tourist dollars and left Vancouver **with** a new transit system. The fair attracted participation **from** 41 countries and 22 million visitors saw Vancouver, many **for** the first time.

9. Skookumchuk Rapids **in** the Chinook Language means "turbulent water." This is just one **of** the many tourist attractions **around** or **in** British Columbia. *(Skookumchuk...what a fantastic name to say, eh?)*

10. A former copper mine **in** Britannia Beach is opened monthly **to** the public and is now a National Historic Site. *(Local school children received free tour tickets at the end of each school year. I went on the tour with our two children in about 1980. It made me much more aware of working conditions for miners. I remember that one machine they showed us over one mile underground (!) was called a "widow-maker." I also remember hoping the tour would end soon!)*

17

Idioms

Idiom   - the grammatical use of a language that is natural to its native speakers

- an expression in a language that cannot be understood from putting together the meanings of the individual words

WORD/IDIOM	DEFINITION
as a matter of fact	actually
better late than never	better to do something late than not at all
blow someone away (to)	amaze/astonish/astound someone
bombed	hammered, loaded, smashed, very drunk
booze	alcohol, liquor
break the bank (to)	spend all of one's savings
breathtaking	beautiful, gorgeous, stunning
bummed out	depressed, sad, unhappy
bundle of nerves (a)	very nervous

burst into tears (to)	start crying suddenly and loudly
butt	cigarette
butt in (to)	cut in, join a line-up at the front or in the middle
call it a day (to)	finish work
carried away	excited or moved to extreme action
chew someone out (to)	reprimand someone harshly
choked up	emotional, upset, tearful
clean up one's act (to)	improve one's behaviour
cost an arm and a leg (to)	very expensive
crack a book (to)	study very hard
cranky	grouchy, grumpy, irritable
dive (a)	terrible, old, dirty place
dough	cash, money
doze off (to)	nap, nod off, sleep, snooze

down and out	very poor, destitute
drink like a fish (to)	consume a lot of alcohol
drop in on someone (to)	visit someone
errand	a short trip to buy groceries, do banking, etc.
face the music (to)	accept the unpleasant results of one's actions
freak out (to)	extremely emotional, upset
get some shut-eye (to)	get some sleep
go back to square one (to)	return to the beginning, start over
go ballistic (to)	furious, livid, very angry
go for it (to)	do it, try it
goof	geek, loser, nerd
gulp down something (to)	drink something quickly
hang a left/right (to)	take a left/right, turn to the left/right

have a crush on someone (to)	be very attracted to someone
have a lump in one's throat (to)	become very emotional, feel like crying
heads up	be alert
hear through the grapevine (to)	hear gossip, hear a rumour
hold your horses (to)	wait, don't go so fast
hit the roof (to)	furious, livid, very angry
in mint condition	in perfect condition, like new
humongous	enormous, gigantic, huge, immense
in the same boat	in the same situation
jerk	terrible person
keep one's fingers crossed (to)	hope for a positive result
kick back (to)	relax, take it easy, get comfortable

knock it off (to)	stop what you are doing, stop it
know like the back of one's hand (to)	be very familiar with something
knuckle down (to)	become serious about one's work
like crazy	actively, fast, very much
lug something (to)	carry something heavy
make a dent in something (to)	make a little progress in something
make do (to)	do one's best with something that is substandard
miss the boat (to)	miss an opportunity or chance
mope around(to)	move around in a sad manner
mull something over (to)	consider, think deeply about something
munchies	snack food
on its last legs	ready to collapse or fail

on the tip of one's tongue	on the verge of remembering something
out of shape	not in top physical health
out of this world	amazing, fantastic, great, unbelievable
pester someone (to)	constantly harass, bother someone, bug
pooped	exhausted, tired, tuckered out, wiped, worn out
pour over something (to)	study very hard, meticulously look at something
pull one's leg (to)	joke, kid around
rant and rave (to)	scream and shout
right up one's alley	perfectly suited to someone
rip-off (a)	overcharged, overpriced
row	fight
safe and sound	safely, unharmed

second wind (a)	catch one's breath, recover from exercise
sharp	exactly, on the dot, very smart
shoot the breeze (to)	chat, gab, talk
short fuse (a)	quick temper, get angry easily
show someone the ropes (to)	show or tell someone how something works
snooze (to)	nap, sleep
something is on me	I'll pay for you, I'll pick up the tab
steep	expensive
stick around (to)	stay
stressed out	more stress than someone can handle
swing by somewhere (to)	stop by somewhere, visit somewhere
tag along with someone (to)	follow someone

take a break (to)	take a rest
take five (to)	take a short break (about 5 minutes)
take in the sights (to)	sightsee, explore, check things out
take off (to)	leave, get going, hit the road
tear-jerker	very sad movie or story
tell someone off (to)	reprimand someone harshly, chew someone out
that goes without saying	that's obvious
time flies	time passes quickly
tonne (a)	a bunch, a load, a lot, a pile, a stack
toss one's cookies (to)	barf, puke, throw up, vomit
turn beet red (to)	blush, turn red in the face
under the weather	sick, ill, unwell
verge (on the)	close to doing, or experiencing something

vivid	colourful, dramatic, vibrant
wander (to)	walk slowly, saunter, stroll
weight off one's shoulders (a)	relief
what's (his/her) face	used when a person's name can't be remembered
wimp	chicken, coward, sissy, wuss
wipe out (to)	fall, crash
wouldn't miss it for the world	would never miss something special
you bet	absolutely, of course
you can say that again	I agree with you

You will find many more idioms here: www.vec.ca/english/11/idioms.cfm

This is just one example of many sites that explain idioms.

18

Weird Canadian Words

Acadian	a French-speaking descendent of the early French settlers in the Maritime Provinces
Alouette	French for skylark (Bird); also the name of a popular French-Canadian song that describes preparing a skylark for cooking
Alouettes	name of the Montréal Canadian Football League (CFL) team
anorak	any heavy, hip-length jacket with a hood; originally made by the Inuit with *waterproof* sealskin; kept many explorers from freezing in the bitter winters; similar to a parka
bakeapples	known by various names in other countries; found in NS and NL; amber coloured and larger than blackberries and raspberries; eaten raw or cooked in pies, jams and liqueurs

beavertails	a deep-fried, flat pastry shaped like a beavertail and topped with either sweet or savoury flavourings – cinnamon sugar, maple butter, garlic butter, etc. See beavertailsinc.com *(Not a dieter's choice!)*
Bluenoser	a person from NS; relates to ruggedness, hardiness and durability, qualities anyone living along the Atlantic coast must possess
Bombardier	the original snowmobile creator and name of the company that is now world famous for its Ski-Doos, Sea-Doos and Lear jets
Bunnyhug	in SK. it's a hooded sweatshirt with a front pocket to keep hands warm; elsewhere in Canada known as a kangaroo or a hoodie
butter tarts	a runny, gooey delicious snack made from a recipe brought to NS by Scottish settlers. Canadians love the taste of brown sugar and raisins in a delicate crust. *(These fit more easily in lunchboxes when made in squares.)*
Canadarm	Canada's first contribution to NASA's space shuttle program; places satellites into orbit and retrieves them for repairs

Canuck	used as an impolite name for French Canadians following the American Revolution; has become a name of pride for both Anglophones and Francophones, although foreigners should not to use the word liberally
Chinook	a warm, dry wind *("snow eater")* that comes down the eastern slopes of the Rockies and brings a brief respite from frigid winter temperatures *(Temperature can rise 20C in one hour!)* See more here: thecanadianencyclopedia.ca/en/article/Chinook/
Cowtown	nickname for Calgary, Alberta, that refers to its roots as a hub of ranching, livestock trade and rodeo culture *(Home of the Calgary Stampede every July)*
Dépanneur	a Québec convenience store, typically family-owned and operated
discombobulated	disorganized, flustered, baffled, befuddled, bewildered, confused
down south	how Canadians refer to the United States of America (USA)

dulse	purply-red seaweed found along the North Atlantic coast of Canada and used as a condiment in soups & stews. *(When dried, it has a salty taste and is great to chew!)*
eh?	used over a thousand years in English and Latin; has meant "something thrown in between." It's used at the end of a statement, basically turning the statement into a rhetorical question and assuming the other person agrees. *(I'd say, "It's cold in Canada, eh?" Then you'd say, "It sure is!")*
Eskimo	used for years for all native inhabitants of the Arctic; replaced in 1970's with Inuit which reflects the true name of the Arctic Aboriginals
Fiddleheads	the furled fronds of a young fern – a food staple for centuries. When steamed or boiled, they acquire a unique grassy and nutty flavor similar to asparagus or artichoke. *(A yummy way to get your 'greens'!)*

First Nations	replaces the term "Indian" (dating back to Christopher Columbus) which Aboriginals found insulting and offensive. The term refers to the tribes of six major cultural regions across Canada; the Woodland First Nations, the Iroquois First Nations, the Plains First Nations, the Plateau First nations, the first Nations of the Pacific Coast and the First Nations of the Mackenzie and Yukon River Basins
gaunch, gitch	gaunch is used in BC & Alberta while gitch is a favourite in Ontario. No one knows why there are so many terms for underwear in Canada! To qualify for the nickname, the undergarment must be a little worn, dirty & smelly! *(No comment here!)*
G'wan and G'way	Maritimes' slang for "Go on" and "Go Away;" an expression meaning "Incredulous!" or "Unbelievable!"
gopher	a short-tailed burrowing rodent with a thickset body, short legs and cute cheek pouches; another name for ground squirrel

Gofer	an employee or assistant whose duties include low-level tasks such as running errands or very thankless work (very slang word)
Grey Cup	the trophy awarded to the victor in the annual football Grey Cup championship game; commissioned by Earl Grey, the Governor General of Canada in 1909.
Habs	historical Québec "Habitants" - nickname of the Montréal Canadians National Hockey League (NHL) team.
had the biscuit	feeling super tired, worn out, "dead tired", broken, spent, exhausted
Hat Trick	in sports, achieving a positive feat three times in a row during a game; e.g.: USA's Carli Lloyd's 3 goals in the 2015 FIFI Women's final soccer game against Japan. A first ever achievement! *(It was an awesome game!)*
huck	to throw or toss something
Islander	person from Prince Edward Island *(Strange, but we don't call someone from Vancouver Island an Islander!)*

IMAX	3 Canadians showed some first-ever multiscreen films at Expo '67 in Montréal; problem was having to use multiple cumbersome projectors. In 1970, at the World's Exposition in Japan, these 3 Canadians showed film on their new invention - the IMAX projector. It reduces the number of slide and film projectors required for audiovisual and multimedia presentations.
Inuksuk	(Inukshuk in English) a stone landmark made by the peoples of the Arctic region from Alaska to Greenland. Used to indicate migration routes; may also mean, "You are on the right path" or "Someone was here."
keener	a person who tries to impress people in authority; one who is overly eager, enthusiastic and intense and who earns the dislike of those around him/her.
klutz	an awkward, clumsy person; often falls down and/or drops things
kokanee salmon	a landlocked freshwater sockeye salmon;
sockeye salmon	are in the Pacific Ocean - when they return upstream to spawn, their backs turn a brilliant red.

coho salmon, or silver salmon, hooknose or sea trout	is native to the Pacific coast. It's a smaller salmon that has been introduced into the Great Lakes. *(A staple food on the west coast and stocks are being depleted.)*
lacrosse	a contact team sport played between two teams using a small rubber ball and a long-handled stick with loose mesh at one end to catch and hold the ball. It was first seen being played by the Aboriginal people in the 1600s. They played with *hundreds* on a team and the game lasted for days! *(Whew!)*
likety-split	going headlong, at full speed, as fast as possible
loonie	the currency of Canada; an 11-sided gold-coloured coin minted in 1987 to replace the one-dollar bill and reduce costs. The image of the loon on one side led to its being nicknamed "the loonie."
Lotus land	used to describe BC with its laid-back and easy-going attitude, its temperate climate, beautiful beaches and closeness to the ocean and the Rocky Mountains; used to imply the difference between the "stressed Easterners" in Central Canada and the easy-going Westerners.

Mainlander	used by people in Newfoundland, PEI and Cape Breton to refer to a person from mainland Canada; often used in the derogatory sense. Also used by Vancouver Island residents, especially Victorians, to refer to residents of the Greater Vancouver/Lower Mainland area rather than those from the Interior or Up-coast.
maple syrup	90% of the syrup in Canada is produced in Québec, drawn from the red maple trees in the Maritimes and south central Canada. Boiling the sap down and when it's "just right" dribbling it over clean snow produces the best tasting taffy. *(As kids we called this "sugar on snow.")*
McIntosh apples	the "Mac" *(not the computer)* has been the most popular apple in Eastern Canada since its discovery by John McIntosh in 1811. It has a tart flavour and is suitable for cooking and eating raw. Apple Inc. employee Jef Raski named the Macintosh line of personal computers after this fruit. *(Yes, it's the computer this time!)*
Minty	in Winnipeg it doesn't have anything to do with spearmint or peppermint. It's an expression that means cool, fantastic or just "in mint condition" – perfect.

mukluk	a knee-high boot – soft, warm and waterproof; originally made from seal skin or reindeer hide; now used to refer to any slipper with a soft sole; can be made from all kinds of synthetic materials.
Nanaimo bar	a dessert square named for the town of Nanaimo, BC and made of egg custard with a Graham-cracker-based bottom and a thin layer of chocolate on top *(But not too thin a layer of chocolate, please!)*
Oka cheese	a semi-soft cheese originally manufactured in 1893 by Trappist monks in Oka, Québec. It has a distinct soft creamy flavour and a sharp aroma;still manufactured in Oka. The story of how it came to Québec is very interesting. Just google Oka Cheese.
Pablum	the first nutritious cereal for infants created in 1931 after 2 years of research by 3 Canadian doctors at the Hospital for Sick Children in Toronto; a mixture of wheat, oats, and vitamins; had a very bland flavour. *(It still has a bland flavour! Yuk! Not bad if mixed with fruit!)*
Parkade	parking garage especially in Western Canada

pencil crayon	coloured pencil
pop	popular name for soft i.e. carbonated drinks or soda pop. *(Could also mean Dad!)*
Potlatch	from Chinook Jargon meaning "to give"; a ceremonial feast among Aboriginal peoples of the northwest Pacific Coast to celebrate a marriage or an accession. Historically, the host of a potlatch distributed gifts according to a guest's rank or status; always with an implicit understanding that the host would be treated the same way when he was a guest.
Poutine	created in Québec in 1957, it combined French fries and cheese curds; eventually gravy was added to the gooey mess; an early French Canadian word from the English word 'pudding.'
RAD	radical, super, neat, radically awesome

Red Rose Tea	a blend of teas from India and Sri Lanka instead of the usual mixture of Chinese and Japanese teas. The new blend soon spread from its company in Saint John, New Brunswick across Canada. A popular TV ad said, "Only in Canada, you say?" Pity."
rez	short for dormitory residences in university or college
runners	running shoes, sneakers (especially in Central Canada)
Screech	short for Newfoundland screech, a potent brand of rum and a traditional drink in the province.
serviette	a small square of cloth or paper used while eating; a napkin
Shivaree	a custom brought to Acadia by the French; a noisy mock serenade given to newlywed couples. *(Sometimes used to just have a party!)*

Sieve	heard often during hockey season to refer to a goalie who lets in too many goals. *(You might hear this comment after a game: "That goalie was such a sieve tonight! No wonder we lost the game, eh?")*
skookum	originally from Chinook Jargon - big, strong and good; now used to refer to something that looks solid, or refers to a good job. It can also mean cool or awesome. *("That's a Skookum winter parka!")*
Snowbirds	refers to people, often senior citizens, who leave Canada during the winter months to live in southern states of USA - particularly Florida; also the name of the Canadian Forces aerobatics team.
Spud Island	an affectionate name for PEI, the province that is Canada's largest supplier of potatoes
Stanfield's	connected with winter and long woolen underwear since 1870. It became famous for a shrink-proof process and the thermal underwear. This affluent Stanfield family seemed like the Kennedys in the USA when Robert Stanfield became Premier of Nova Scotia 1956-1967.

Stanley Cup	created in 1893 when Lord Stanley, Governor General of Canada, bought a silver punch bowl to award to the top amateur Canadian hockey team. He hoped to increase hockey's popularity beyond Québec and Ontario. It quickly became the symbol of hockey excellence and supremacy and every member of the winning team gets to take the cup home for a day.
Stubble jumper	someone/farmer from a prairie province. (Stubble is the stiff, 12-inch end of a wheat or hay plant after harvesting).
take off	expression of disagreement or command to leave, similar to "get lost"
Tim Horton's	affectionately called "Timmy's" or "Tim's,"- Canada's largest quick service restaurant chain founded in 1964 by Ontario hockey player Tim Horton & partner, Jim Charade. It has twice as many outlets as McDonalds and holds 62% of the Canadian coffee market. (Starbucks is in number two position with 7%). *(Not bad for an old hockey player, eh?)*

Timbits	Tim Horton's brand name of donut holes; also the general name of Minor Hockey Teams that are sponsored by Tim Horton's
toboggan	a simple snow sled, a traditional form of transport used by the Inuit & Cree of northern Canada; a long narrow sled, with wooden boards curved upwards at one end; today used to carry mostly children down a slope for fun in the snow. *(Most adults can't resist a toboggan ride!)*
Toonie	in 1996 the new coin replaced the paper two-dollar bill. On one side a polar bear crosses an ice floe in early summer to show the diversity of geography and weather in Canada. Britain's Queen Elizabeth's picture is on the other side .
Tourtiére	a traditional Québec meat pie served usually at the Christmas Eve feast or réveillon, after midnight Mass or on New Year's Eve. Each region of Québec has its own special recipe with beef, pork, lamb, veal or venison with a mixture of spices, especially cinnamon and cloves.

Toutin	a dough cake or flapjack, a popular breakfast item in NL. Allowed to rest overnight, the dough is then cut into bite-sized pieces and fried in pork fat, then covered with molasses and bits of pork.
Towney	in NL describes someone from St. John's. The term can also be heard in BC by rural residents to refer to town residents nearby.
Tuque/toque	a knitted sock-like cap, possibly invented by European sailors to keep their heads warm on long ocean voyages. The word may have come from the French verb toquer "to knock" (the original tuque had a long, drooping end that tended to knock its wearer on the back of the neck.) The word may also have come from the Chinook Jargon word latuk, meaning "woolen cap". See a picture in Chapter 4 *(No Canadian closet should be without one!)*
Vi-Co	originally a brand of malted chocolate milk, it is now used mainly in Saskatchewan to refer to all chocolate milk. A variation of the White Russian drink, is made with vodka, ice and Vi-Co and is know as the "Psycho Vi-Co."
washroom, loo, bathroom, restroom	a public place for toilets and washbasins.

wheels	referring to method of transportation, usually a car
whisky jack	or moosebird, camp robber or Canada jay. Watch out while resting with a snack in the woods. These jays will swoop down and empty your hands! They eat anything edible – and some things not so edible!
WonderBra	created in 1964 by Canadian designer Louise Poirier for the Canadian lingerie company Canadelle. Its 54 design elements underlined its full name: The WonderBra Push-Up Plunge Bra. It came to USA in 1994 and was on the year's Top Ten products lists in *Fortune, Time, Newsweek* and *USA Today*. *(We Canadians are not just known for maple syrup and hockey, eh?)*
Zipper	used to bind the edges of an opening of fabric or other material, as on a garment or a bag. A "clasp locker," first seen at the Chicago World's Fair in 1893, didn't become popular until 1923. That's when the B.F. Goodrich Company bought 150,000 of them. What would a tire manufacturer want with a "hookless fastener"? Was it an American or Canadian who invented the zipper as we know it? Google 'zipper' and you decide!

19

Resources

Pg 2 L'Anse aux Meadows - Paul Illsley, Photographer. Paul generously allowed me to use his photo of this historical icon, and also his picture of the Sambro Lighthouse (Pg. 40) See more beautiful images of the Maritimes here: paulillsley.com

Pg. 7 In the Northland by Tom Thomson – Thanks to the Montreal Museum of Fine Arts for permission to use this beautiful picture from their collection: mbam.qc.ca
The Montreal Museum of Fine Arts, purchase, gift of Dr. Francis J. Shepherd, Sir Vincent Meredith, Drs. Lauterman and W. Gardner and Mrs. Hobart Molson. Photo: Denis Farley.

Pg. 13 Sir Wilfred Grenfell - Pierre Berton narrates this 54-minute video – great NL footage! youtube.com/watch?v=1nPWjy3ECLU

Sir Wilfred Grenfell – enjoy this short video clip on his life in Newfoundland and Labrador: youtube.com/watch?v=wD-i_86GDGI

Pg. 15 The rows of brightly coloured Victorian row-houses are affectionately known as "Jellybean Row." You can see them in the hit CBC TV series, *Republic of Doyle*. Just Google "Houses in St. John's" to learn more

Pg. 17 A whaler's boat - on display in the visitor centre of Red Bay National Historic Site of Canada. Explore the Red Bay site:

  pc.gc.ca/eng/lhn-nhs/nl/redbay/index.aspx

Pg. 21 NONIA – The Newfoundland Outport Nursing and Industrial Association was founded in 1920 to assist outport communities to access health services. See the beautiful handcrafts at the NONIA shop at 286 Water Street in St. John's and more here: NONIA.com

Pg. 27   BC Delicious – painting by Mary Pratt – Used with permission of Equinox Gallery, Vancouver, BC. Google "jelly shelf" to see more exquisite paintings.

Pg. 29   Fiddleheads – Thanks to Niamh Shields for permission to use this right-from-the-earth picture! Check out the tempting recipes *(I'm trying the Goan Prawn Curry tonight!)* and beautiful places this traveller has been! All here: www.eatlikeagirl.com

Pg. 34   Hartland Bridge - built in 1901, was considered an amazing engineering feat, rather like how the Confederation Bridge between NB & PEI is acclaimed today.

Pg. 37   Lobster Sculpture – I have to say that "lobster mania" occurs across Canada in the summer. I have even bought a lobster roll in Subway in BC with Atlantic lobster shipped from "back East." *(The server wasn't sure where back East but it tasted like NB to me!)*

Pg. 37   Hopewell Rocks – Enjoy these pictures because as this book goes to print, the great "elephant" rock has recently split and this has changed the historical look of these flowerpots. See pictures and read more here: cbc.ca/news/canada/new-brunswick/hopewell-rocks-elephant-collapse-1.3492174

Pg. 50   PEI Boardwalk – courtesy of the NS Ramblers Bicycle Club. Thanks to President, Sandra Bennett, for permission to use this image. See more here: nsramblers.squarespace.com/

Pg. 61   Bonhomme Carnaval – created in 1954 as the "mascot" for the Québec Winter Carnival - the largest winter carnival in the world. See more here: carnaval.qc.ca/carnaval/our-history

Pg. 73   Autumn Hillside (1920) by Franklin Carmichael – © Public Domain. Read about the Group of Seven and see their wonderful paintings here: wikiart.org/en/franklin-carmichael/autumn-hillside-1920

Pp. 74 & 75   CN Tower – These 2 images are courtesy of CN Tower. See more here: cntower.ca

Pg. 92   Grain Elevator - Many thanks to Glenn Cameron for permission to use this image of a disappearing Canadian icon. Check: roadstories.ca to see *"The People, Places and Things that make Canada great… a place where Canada-lovers can share their affection for this gigantic piece of geography and the people who call her 'home.'"*

Pg. 103   This awesome picture is only one of the many tours you may take in Alberta. For more pictures and how to book your own adventure go here:

whitewaterraftingjasper.com

Pg. 104   Steer-roping – Thanks to Christopher Martin, for permission to use this awesome picture. See more breath-taking images here:

christophermartinphotography.com

Pg. 113   The Last Spike – Royal BC Museum and Archives image E02200. Learn more about BC Archives here:

royalbcmuseum.bc.ca/bcarchives/

Pg. 114   Douglas Fir Tree – Courtesy of the Wilderness Committee files

"The Wilderness Committee is Canada's largest membership-based wilderness preservation group with 60,000 members, supporters and volunteers. Founded in 1980, we've help gain protection for over 60 major wilderness areas in Canada, including millions of hectares of critical wildlife habitats and some of the world's last tract of old-growth temperate rainforest and boreal forest." Learn more here: wildernesscommittee.org

Pg. 119   Totem Poles in an Aboriginal Village by Emily Carr – Royal BC Museum and Archives image PDP00612. See more of Emily Carr's work here: royalbcmuseum.bc.ca

Pg. 125 Mount Logan – Canada's highest mountain. Used with permission from David Hik, Professor, Department of Biological Sciences, University of Alberta. See the newly-formed website: canadianmountainnetwork.ca to learn more about how this group is working for *"the sustainability of our mountain spaces and those communities who inhabit them."* Also view these sites for more information on our First Nations northern communities:

travelyukon.com/About/First-Nation-Culture
cyfn.ca
kfn.ca

Pg. 127   Yukon Black Bear – Used with permission from Amanda Harris of Southern Comfort Photography. Visit the wonderful photo galleries: southerncomfortphotography.com. Then check this website for a short video on the Yukon – awesome pictures including the northern lights!

discoveryyukon.com

Pg. 137   Polar Bear - Gratefully used with permission: JSGrove.com

Pg. 138   NWT Legislative Building – Wikimedia commons. Photo by Hldeyukl Kamon

Pg. 144   Inuit Village – Used with gratitude and permission of John Rich

Pg. 151   Beluga Whale – Photograph by Nansen Weber, shot at Arctic Watch Wilderness Lodge. For a short tour of the Arctic Wilderness go here:

Arcticwatch.ca/gallery/

The Arctic is such a fitting place to finish this book. Hearing whales "singing" and seeing a land like no other, will surely touch your heart and soul.

Author's Notes

* Because Canada uses the metric system I did not convert any measurements to the imperial system. However, for my USA readers (and others!) here is an easy conversion site: metric-conversions.org/converter.htm

* Unless otherwise noted, all population numbers are from the 2011 Canadian Census. The 2016 Census figures are not yet available.

* I did not include information on governments, either federal, provincial or territorial as there is excellent information on many internet sites. To learn more about Canada's Parliament and system of government here are two of many online sites for you to explore:

   parl.gc.ca   and canadaonline.about.com/od/parliament/

* To test your knowledge of Canada and to see examples of questions for a Canadian Citizenship exam, you will find helpful information here:

   yourlibrary.ca/citizenship/

20

Watercolour Flowers - Jane Crosby, Artist

The provincial and territorial flowers in this book are from original watercolour paintings by *Jane Crosby*.

Jane is an artist living in Vancouver, Canada. After devoting over thirty years to a rewarding career in health care, her life has been transformed by watercolour painting. Her favourite subjects are flowers and vintage teacups, often done in fine detail, although she also enjoys doing occasional portraits or landscapes.

Jane is an Active Member of the Federation of Canadian Artists, and has shown her works at a number of venues in Vancouver. She has studied at the British Columbia Institute of Technology, Simon Fraser University, and Emily Carr University of Art and Design.

Jane loves painting in the sanctuary of her home studio. When not in her studio, she enjoys tending her garden, reading, travelling, and spending time with her husband, family, friends, and two dogs.

Jane's website is www.janecrosby.com

CPSIA information can be obtained
at www.ICGtesting.com
Printed in the USA
LVHW07s0055010618
579128LV00022B/292/P